# NORSE MYTHOLOGY
## A TO Z

# NORSE MYTHOLOGY
# A TO Z

Revised Edition

Kathleen N. Daly
Revised by Marian Rengel

☑®
Facts On File, Inc.

**Norse Mythology A to Z, Revised Edition**

Copyright © 2004, 1991 by Kathleen N. Daly

Facts On File, Inc.
132 West 31st Street
New York NY 10001

**Library of Congress Cataloging-in-Publication Data**
Daly, Kathleen N.
Norse mythology A to Z / Kathleen N. Daly ; revised by
Marian Rengel. — Rev. ed.
p. cm. — (Mythology A to Z)
Summary: Alphabetically listed entries identify and explain the characters, events, and important places of Norse mythology.
Includes bibliographical references and index.
ISBN 0-8160-5156-9 (alk. paper)
1. Mythology, Norse—Dictionaries, Juvenile. [1. Mythology, Norse—Dictionaries.]
I. Rengel, Marian. II. Title.
BL850.D34 2003
293′.13—dc21
2003045758

Facts On File books are available at special discounts when purchased in bulk quantities for businesses, associations, institutions, or sales promotions. Please call our Special Sales Department in New York at (212) 967-8800 or (800) 322-8755.

You can find Facts On File on the World Wide Web at http://www.factsonfile.com

Text design by Joan Toro
Cover design by Cathy Rincon
Map by Jeremy Eagle

Printed in the United States of America

VB Hermitage 10 9 8 7 6 5 4 3 2 1

This book is printed on acid-free paper.

*To my own favorite Norse people and their families*
*(in alphabetical order):*
*Helen, Jorgen, Kirsten and Ole*

*— K.N.D.*

# CONTENTS

# INTRODUCTION

## WHAT IS A MYTH?

Myths are as ancient as humankind and have their origin in the efforts of primitive people to explain the mysteries of the world around them: thunder and lightning; floods and fire; rain and drought; earthquakes and volcanic eruptions; night and day; the Sun, Moon, and stars; the seasons; the existence of plants and animals, man and woman; and birth and death. Myths fulfill a need in people to believe in some higher being or beings who have power over the daily lives and fate of humankind. Many of the world's myth systems include a sky god or father of all and an earth mother. In many cases, including the myths of the Norse, people believed in a set of attendant gods and goddesses, as well as villains such as demons, dragons, and other monsters; giants and dwarfs; and supernatural forces.

Myths help people structure their lives. The myths reflect their codes of behavior, their cultural customs and rites, and their ways of worship. Myths are basically stories of the struggle between good and evil, between order and chaos. They foretell of the eventual breakdown of order, but also of regeneration.

Ancient myths about the creation of the universe and the living creatures on Earth were passed orally from one generation to another, from family to family, and from one community to another. The stories changed according to the whim of the narrator, for it was thousands of years before the stories were written down. As people moved from one part of a continent to another, they adapted their stories to the changing landscape or climate. Stories that may have originated in India, the Middle East, or the south of Europe changed dramatically when people told them in the harsh, craggy, icy lands of the north, where summers were short and winters long and cruel.

Finally, myths are part of a moral and ethical, often spiritual, belief system. Many historians of myths and scholars of human social development see myths as part of a religious belief system and an attempt to explain human existence.

## WHO WERE THE NORSE?

The Norse (people of the north) are known today as the Scandinavians—the people of Norway, Sweden, Denmark, Iceland, and the Faeroe Islands.

Mistakenly, Norsemen are often thought of only as the fierce warriors of the Viking Age (A.D. 780–1070); however, Norse culture originated long before the dramatic explorations of the Vikings. It probably started to take root during the Bronze Age (1600–450 B.C.). No written sources describe early Norse culture, but surviving works in metal and stone depict gods and goddesses and provide glimpses of ancient myths and rituals. The Norse were superb shipbuilders and navigators, intrepid explorers, and people with a strong sense of family and clan loyalty. They also loved a good story, a quick wit, and fine craftsmanship, which we can see in the ancient carvings, weaponry, and utensils that have been discovered in a variety of archaeological sites across Scandinavia. The mythology of these strong, lively people was rich, vigorous, and clever.

Norse mythology originated, according to experts, in Asia, was modified in the European Mediterranean lands, and eventually was carried north and west by migrating Teutonic tribes, in the third to sixth centuries A.D. during the breakup of the Roman Empire. The roaming tribes included Angles and Saxons, Goths, Visigoths and Ostrogoths, Alemanni, Vandals, Franks, and others. As the migrating tribes settled, the old stories they brought with them began to change with the local geography, climate, and temperament of the people. Later, during the Viking Age, the Norse began to explore and populate countries from the British Isles and the rest of Europe to Iceland, America, the Near East, Byzantium, and Russia, taking with them, too, their myths and their culture.

The Norse myths were not written down, however, until the 13th century, by which time Christianity was established in northern Europe and had displaced paganism, that is, the worship and the myths of the

Rock carvings of the earliest Norse ships, from Norway and Sweden *(New York Public Library Picture Collection)*

ancient gods. Thus much of the ancient lore is lost to modern audiences. What remains is fragmented, incomplete, and often distorted by the pious Christian monks who edited the pagan tales as they transcribed them onto parchment for the first time. Although the Norse myths as we know them today are often confusing and contradictory, they still present us with wonderful tales about these northern people.

## THE SOURCES OF THE NORSE MYTHS
The main sources of the Norse myths are

- poetry of the early skalds (poets) transmitted orally until the 13th century
- *Poetic Edda*, a collection of verses written by different poets at different times between the eighth and 13th centuries
- *Prose Edda*, a handbook written by the Icelandic poet scholar, historian, and diplomat Snorri Sturluson, around 1220
- *Gesta Danorum*, written by Danish historian Saxo Grammaticus about 1215
- historical observations by Roman author Tacitus, notably in *Germania* (end of the first century A.D.), the Arab traveler Ibn Fadlan (10th century A.D.), and the German historian Adam of Bremen (11th century A.D.)
- *Landnamabok (Book of Settlements)*, from the 13th century A.D.
- the 13th-century Icelandic sagas (about 700 of them), written by unknown authors, which are a valuable source of information about pre-Christian beliefs and practices, kings and bishops, Norse exploration and settlement, and legendary heroes such as Sigurd the Volsung

## HOW TO USE THIS BOOK
The entries in this book are in alphabetical order and may be looked up as you would use a dictionary. In case you are not familiar with the Norse myths, here is a list of the chief characters and the stories in which they are most important. If you look up the entries concerning these characters, you will find a general overview of Norse mythology. The index at the back of the book will help you find the following stories and characters and many more. Within the main text cross-references to other entries are printed in SMALL CAPITAL letters. Some topics with entries in this book are known by more than one name. Alternate names are given in parentheses after the entry headword. Those given in full capital letters are variations of the names from the original language; those appearing in upper- and lowercase letters are English translations.

First the gods:

**ODIN**  The one-eyed god, the All-Father, the god of wisdom and poetry, of war and death. Odin plays a principal role in many of the

An ancient depiction of Thor *(New York Public Library Picture Collection)*

myths including those of the CREATION, the WAR BETWEEN THE AESIR AND THE VANIR, "The Death of Balder" (SEE BALDER), and RAGNAROK, the end of the world.

**THOR**   God of thunder, son of ODIN and FRIGG. He was the strongest of the gods, of fiery temper but well loved. He had a hammer (MJOLLNIR), a magic belt (MEGINGJARDIR), and iron gauntlets and was forever at war with the giants.

**LOKI**   A mischievous god, Loki is involved in many of the myths. Loki often deceives the gods and creates dangerous situations and then comes to the rescue of the gods. He is admired yet distrusted by them.

**BALDER**   Son of ODIN and FRIGG. He was the most beautiful and beloved of the gods. There is only one myth about him but it is one of the best known.

**NIORD**    A VANIR god of the seas and seafarers. Niord has two major roles in the myths: as a hostage sent to ASGARD, the home of the AESIR gods, along with the twin deities FREY and FREYA, his children; and as the husband of the giantess SKADE.

**FREY**    A VANIR god, sent to ASGARD as a hostage along with his twin sister, FREYA, and his father, NIORD. Frey was a god of fertility, peace, and plenty, and was much worshiped.

**TYR**    One of the most ancient gods and the most mysterious, he was also the bravest and most just of the gods when he undertook to put his hand into the jaws of the terrible wolf, FENRIR.

**BRAGI**    Called the god of poetry, he was a minor figure in the surviving myths.

**HEIMDALL**    The watchman of the gods who guarded BIFROST, the bridge that connected ASGARD (the domain of the gods) with MIDGARD (the Middle Earth). Heimdall had a trumpet, GIALAR, with which he would summon the gods to battle at RAGNAROK.

The goddesses play a lesser role in the surviving Norse myths, according to extant manuscripts, but scholars believe they were important to the people who practiced Norse religion.

**FRIGG**    The wife of ODIN. Her greatest role is in the myth of BALDER, her beloved son, whom she tries to protect from death.

**FREYA**    The goddess of fertility, the twin sister of FREY, and the daughter of NIORD. She is beautiful and has a fatal love of gold. She is loved by DWARFS and giants alike. She may have been acquainted with magic and prophecy, but few facts are known about her.

**IDUNN**    The keeper of the apples of youth, she is known only through the myth "Idunn and the Golden Apples" (see IDUNN).

Other females in Norse mythology are the NORNS and the VALKYRIES. The Norns are the three Fates who represent the past, the present, and the future and who determine the destiny of all living creatures. The Norns are more powerful even than the gods.

The Valkyries are Odin's warrior maidens who select the fallen heroes and carry them to Odin's hall, VALHALLA.

The forces of evil are represented chiefly by the offspring of Loki: HEL, queen of death and the underworld; FENRIR, the monster wolf; and JORMUNGAND, the Midgard Serpent who is so huge that he encircles the Earth and holds his tail in his mouth. Other wolves chase after the Sun and the Moon, and numerous JOTUNS try to outwit and outfight the gods.

ARCTIC OCEAN

ICELAND

Reykjavík

Surtsey

ATLANTIC
OCEAN

0    50 Miles
0    50 Kms

N

FAEROE
ISLANDS
(DENMARK)

ATLANTIC
OCEAN

N

ARCTIC OCEAN

Norwegian
Sea

NORWAY

Hegge

Hallingdal R.

HALLINGDAL

Oslo

SETESDAL

Oseberg

Kalnes

SWEDEN

Lake
Vänern

Lake
Vättern

Gulf of Bothnia

UPPLAND

Uppsala

Stockholm

Gotland

Alskog
Tjangvide

North
Sea

Skagerrak

DENMARK

Dejberg

JUTLAND

Jelling

Egtved

Sjaelland
(Zealand)

Copenhagen

Baltic Sea

N

0    200 Miles
0    200 Kms

✦ Archaeological site

# A-to-Z Entries

# A

**AEGIR** The JOTUN lord of the sea. He was married to his sister, RAN, and was the father of nine daughters, the waves, who were said to be the mothers of the god HEIMDALL. Some stories say that Aegir was the brother of LOKI and Kari (Air). He belonged to a primeval order of gods, predating the AESIR, the VANIR, and the GIANTS, DWARFS, and ELVES. Aegir is usually pictured as an old man with long white hair and clawlike hands. His dwelling is on the island of HLESEY, in coral caves beneath the land. His servants are ELDIR and FIMAFENG.

In Anglo-Saxon mythology Aegir was called Eagor. Whenever an unusually large wave approached men at sea, they cried, "Look out, Eagor is coming!" Supposedly, in ancient Saxon times one of every 10 prisoners was sacrificed to Eagor to ensure that the raiders would return safely home.

See also "Loki's Mocking," under LOKI, which takes place at a banquet in Aegir's hall; "Otr's Ransom," under OTR, in which Loki borrows Ran's fishing net; and "Thor and Hymir Go Fishing," under THOR, in which Thor and TYR bring back a cauldron that Aegir uses to brew ale for the feasting of the gods.

**AESIR** The race of gods who lived in ASGARD under the leadership of the chief god, ODIN. Other gods included BALDER, the beautiful; BRAGI, god of poetry; FORSETI, god of justice; FREY, god of fertility; HEIMDALL, the watchman of the gods; NIORD, the sea god; THOR, god of thunder; TYR, a brave sky god; ULL, a winter god; VALI, the avenger; and VIDAR, the silent god.

Not many myths survive about the goddesses except for those concerning FREYA, the fertility goddess; FRIGG, wife of Odin; IDUNN, keeper of the apples of youth; and SIF, the golden-haired wife of Thor (see ASYNJUR).

**AGNAR** Son of HRAUDING and brother of GEIR-ROD (2). When he and his brother were shipwrecked, they were befriended by an old couple who were ODIN and FRIGG in disguise. Frigg took special care of Agnar, who was eventually betrayed by his brother, Odin's protegé. In later years another Agnar (probably the son of Geirrod) took pity on Odin, who had been captured and slung between two fires. After Agnar had given Odin ale to quench his thirst, Odin chanted a song that was known as the GRIMNISMAL.

**ALFODR** (All-Father) A name for ODIN used frequently in the *POETIC EDDA*, SKALDIC POETRY, and SNORRI STURLUSON's work. Odin is recognized as the father of all the AESIR gods and goddesses, but he has this role in name only. He is also known as the father of all dead warriors. In addition Odin can be considered the father of all human beings, for when Odin and his brothers, VILI and VE, found the shapes of the first man and woman, ASK and EMBLA, on a beach, they gave them the spirit, mental powers, and warmth they needed to become fully human.

**ALFRIGG** One of the four DWARFS who made the BRISINGAMEN for the goddess FREYA. The others were BERLING, DVALIN, and GRERR.

**ALSVID** (ALSVIN; All-Swift) One of two horses that draw the Sun's chariot, driven by the fair maiden SOL. The other horse is ARVAKR.

**ALSVIDER** (Rapid Goer) The horse that pulled the Moon's chariot for MANI.

**ALVIS** (All-Wise) A DWARF, tricked by THOR, who was turned to stone. Alvis had come to ASGARD to claim the bride (perhaps THRUD, daughter of the god THOR) whom the gods had promised him. Thor, knowing that Alvis, like many dwarfs, liked to show off his considerable knowledge, lured the dwarf into a lengthy question-and-answer game. Thor asked Alvis for alternative names for the 13 words that were most important in the lives of medieval Scandinavians. These names the dwarf gave according to the four main groups of beings that inhabited the worlds of Norse mythology. Alvis talked as the night wore on. At the end the Sun, which the dwarf had called "DVALIN'S DELIGHT," came up and turned Alvis to stone, as was the fate of all dwarfs caught in the sunlight.

The 13 words for which Alvis gave alternative names are given in the *Lay of Alvis* (*Alvismal*) in the *Prose Edda*. They are as follows:

**Alvis Answers with**

| Thor Asks About | Men | Gods | Giants | Dwarfs and Elves |
|---|---|---|---|---|
| Earth | Earth | fields, ways | evergreen place | growing place, clay |
| heaven | heaven | warmer of the heights | wind weaver | high home, fair roof, dripping hall |
| Moon | Moon | mock Sun | night traveler | month teller, gleamer, whirling wheel |
| Sun | Sun, Sol | shining orb | ever-bright | fair wheel, Dvalin's delight |
| clouds | sky, skies | shower bringers | wind floes, wind kites | rain bearers, weather tellers, helmets of darkness |
| wind | wind | waverer, noise-maker | whooper, wailer | roaring traveler, blusterer |

**Alvis Answers with**

| Thor Asks About | Men | Gods | Giants | Dwarfs and Elves |
|---|---|---|---|---|
| calm | calm | quietness | wind's husk | sultry, day's lull, day's refuge |
| main | sea | home of waves | home of eels | the big drink, the deep |
| fire | fire | flamer | greedy one | furnace, burner, destroyer |
| wood | wood | shelter of the fields | fuel | fair limbs, adorner of the hills |
| night | night | darkness | day's mask | unlight, soother, bringer of dreams |
| seed | barley | grain, grower | food maker | slender stalk maker |
| ale | ale | beer, foamer | swill | good cheer, mead |

**AMSVARTNIR**   The lake in which stood the island of LYNGVI, where the gods bound the wolf FENRIR.

**ANDHRIMNIR** (Sooty Faced)   The cook at VALHALLA, whose job it was to roast the magic boar, SAEHRIMNIR, each night for the feasting of the gods and heroes.

**ANDVARANAUT** (Andvari's Loom)   The magic ring LOKI stole from the dwarf ANDVARI. The ring worked like a magnet to attract gold (see "Otr's Ransom," under OTR).

**ANDVARI**   The DWARF whom LOKI, the trickster god, robs of his hoard of gold. Andvari had put a curse upon his treasure, including the ring, which was called ANDVARANAUT. Loki gave the treasure to the magician HREIDMAR in compensation for killing his son OTR.

**ANGRBODA** (Bringer of Distress)  The ogress wife of LOKI and mother of the wolf FENRIR; HEL, the goddess of death; and JORMUNGAND, the Midgard Serpent.

Angrboda may also be the same as AURBODA and thus the mother of GERDA and the wife of the giant GYMIR.

**ANNAR** (Second, Another)  A giant and the second husband of NOTT. Their daughter was FJORGYN (1) (Earth).

SNORRI STURLUSON also refers to a distant ancestor of THOR and SIF named Annar in the prologue to GYLFAGINNING.

**APPLE**  The apple tree is common throughout the temperate regions of the world. The tree and its fruit symbolize love, fertility, and youth in many mythologies, including the Norse (see "Idunn's Apples," under IDUNN) and the Greek (for example, the tale of Paris and the apple of discord).

**ARVAKR** (Early Waker)  One of two horses that drew the Sun's chariot across the sky for the fair maiden SOL. The other horse was ALSVID.

**ASGARD**  The realm of the AESIR gods. ODIN presides over Asgard, the topmost level of the NINE WORLDS. Here the gods and goddesses had their palaces and mansions, called halls. Asgard was surrounded and protected by a mighty wall constructed by the GIANT MASTER BUILDER. In the center of Asgard was the green field IDAVOLL, around which stood the 13 halls of the gods: Among them were GLADSHEIM, the main hall of the gods; BILSKIRNIR, the hall of THOR; FENSALIR, which belonged to FRIGG; BREIDABLIK, where BALDER and his wife, NANNA, lived; HIMINBJORG, the abode of HEIMDALL; GLITNIR, where FORSETI presided; SESSRUMNIR, FREYA's hall; and VALHALLA, where Odin entertained the slain heroes of the world. BIFROST, the Rainbow Bridge, connected Asgard to MIDGARD (Middle Earth). At RAGNAROK, the end of the world, all the beautiful mansions would be destroyed, but the golden playthings of the gods—chess pieces—would remain, and a new world would arise.

**Asgard's Wall and the Giant Master Builder**
The Aesir gods wanted to build a new wall around their stronghold, Asgard. The VANIR had destroyed the original wall in the first and last battle between the two races of gods (see WAR BETWEEN THE AESIR AND THE VANIR).

The gods were good at building fine halls and glittering palaces, but to build a fortresslike wall seemed an enormous task.

One day a large man trotted his horse over Bifrost, the Rainbow Bridge, and told Heimdall, the watchman god, that he had a plan to put before the gods. Heimdall reported the news to the chief god, Odin, who assembled all the gods and goddesses together to meet the stranger.

The tall man, who was a giant in disguise, said that he would rebuild the wall around Asgard in 18 months. For his fee, Giant Master Builder would take the goddess Freya to be his wife. He would also take the SUN AND MOON.

The gods roared with anger. Odin said that he would never part with beautiful Freya nor with the Sun and the Moon, which gave warmth and light to the world. He ordered the mason to leave.

LOKI, the sly god, begged the other gods not to be hasty and asked the mason for some time to consider his plan. The mason left the hall, and the gods and goddesses clustered around Loki while Freya began to weep tears of gold.

Loki suggested that if they could get the mason to promise to build the wall in six months—before springtime—they would have nothing to fear, for obviously it was impossible for anyone to complete the wall so quickly. But at least the mason could dig the foundation and get a good start on the wall, thus saving the gods a lot of work. And, said Loki, they would not have to pay him a thing.

Odin called the builder back into the hall and told him their decision. At first the mason seemed dismayed by how little time he would have to finish the work, but at last he agreed to try, provided that he could have his great stallion, SVADILFARI, to help him. They struck a bargain.

As the giant began to build the wall, the gods looked on in amazement. Never had they seen a man cut such huge blocks of stone, nor a horse pull such heavy loads. The wall began to take shape, getting higher and higher and stronger and stronger. Though the winter was cruel, the tall man labored on undaunted.

At last the cold and the snow and the ice abated. The last day of winter was near, and the wall was almost finished.

The gods met again. If the mason finished the wall in time, they would lose their treasured Freya and the Sun and the Moon. Suddenly they wondered how they had arrived at this terrible predicament. Then they remembered. They threw dark looks at Loki.

Odin commanded Loki to use his cunning once again, this time to save the goddess Freya and the Sun and the Moon. Terrified of Odin's anger, Loki promised that he would find a way to outwit the builder.

That evening, as the mason led Svadilfari toward the pile of stones to be hauled, the stallion pranced gaily. He could smell spring in the air. Suddenly he spied a beautiful young mare. She danced up to him and swished her tail. It was more than Svadilfari could stand. With a mighty bound he broke free of his harness and bolted after the mare.

The mason shouted with rage and set off in pursuit, but it was useless. Svadilfari had worked through a long, lonely winter, and now he wanted some light-hearted fun with the pretty mare.

Dawn came and with it the end of winter.

The wall stood unfinished. The mason lost the bargain and was slain by the thunder god, Thor.

When Loki returned to Asgard several months later, he led a handsome young colt. It had eight legs and obviously would grow up to be a magnificent horse. Indeed, its father was the mighty Svadilfari, and its mother was none other than Loki himself, who had disguised himself as the pretty mare. Odin claimed the colt for his own and named it SLEIPNIR, the glider.

This myth shows the enmity between the gods and the giants—a theme that occurs in most Norse myths and does not end until Ragnarok. When the giant demands the Sun and the Moon and also Freya, he intends to deprive the gods not only of the four seasons but also of the possibility of regeneration, for Freya was the goddess of love and fertility.

The only complete version of this myth is in SNORRI STURLUSON's *PROSE EDDA*.

**ASH** A tree of the olive family (genus *Fraxinus*). In Norse mythology the ash, or YGGDRASIL, is considered sacred and is called the World Tree as it plays a dominant part in the makeup of the NINE WORLDS.

The AESIR gods created the first man, ASK, by breathing life into the trunk of an ash tree (see also "The First Humans," under CREATION).

**ASK** The first man, created from the trunk of an ASH tree by the first three AESIR gods, ODIN, VILI, and VE (see "The First Humans," under CREATION). All human beings, it is said in Norse mythology, are descended from Ask and EMBLA, the first woman.

**ASYNJUR** (ASYNJER) The AESIR goddesses, the female form of the word *Aesir*. The most prominent Asynjur was FRIGG, wife of ODIN, who was goddess of love, marriage, and motherhood. The 13th-century chronicler of NORSE myths SNORRI STURLUSON named 20 Asynjur in two separate lists. They are Bil, EIR, FREYA, Frigg, FULLA, GEFION, GERDA, GNA, HLIN, IDDUN, LOFN, NANNA, SAGA (2), SIGYN, SJOFN, SNOTRA, SOL, SYN, VAR, and VOR. Many of these goddesses are considered by scholars to be handmaidens of Frigg.

Snorri does not include among the Asynjur the more dominant goddesses, SIF, wife of THOR, or SKADE, wife of NIORD.

**AUD** (Wealth) The son of NOTT and her first husband, NAGLFARI. Aud is named and referred to only in the works of SNORRI STURLUSON.

**AUDHUMLA** The first cow, formed at the CREATION of the world. Audhumla appeared at the same time as YMIR, the first giant, and fed him with her milk. She herself derived nourishment by licking the salty stones around GINNUNGAGAP, the primeval abyss. As she licked, she uncovered a handsome, man-like creature from the ice. He was BURI, the first ancestor of the gods.

In many mythologies the cow is a symbol of the Great Mother and of creation. Audhumla appears in the *PROSE EDDA* and in the *POETIC EDDA*.

**AURBODA**   The mother of the giantess GERDA. Aurboda was possibly another name for ANGRBODA.

**AURORA BOREALIS**   Shimmering lights or luminescence that sometimes appear in night skies in the Northern Hemisphere. Also called the northern lights. In Norse mythology this beautiful sight was said to be the radiance emitted by GERDA, the JOTUN maiden who became the wife of the god FREY.

**AURVANDIL**   Known as The Brave, he was the husband of the seer GROA. Not much is known about Aurvandil except that the god THOR rescued him from the giants and carried him across the poisonous rivers of ELIVAGAR in a basket. One of Aurvandil's toes froze. Thor plucked it off and threw it into the sky, where it shone forevermore as the bright star Aurvandil's toe. (We do not know today which star it is.)

**AUSTRI** (East)   One of the four DWARFS named after the cardinal compass directions. The others are VESTRI (West), NORDI (North), and SUDRI (South). Though these four dwarfs are mentioned in early Norse poetry, it was Icelandic poet SNORRI STURLUSON who gave Austri and his three companions the job of holding up the four corners of the sky.

Austri is a name used often in Norse poetry. In some cases the name refers to a person involved in a conflict who is smaller and weaker than his opponent. In others it refers to the dwarfs who surrendered their MEAD, a strong alcoholic drink, to the giant SUTTUNG. In yet another use Austri refers to the dwarf who steered a ship filled with dwarfs.

# B

**BALDER** The beloved son of the great god ODIN and his wife, FRIGG. The story of the god Balder is one of the most famous and one of the most complete in Norse mythology. It has been retold many times over the centuries, from SNORRI STURLUSON's account in the *PROSE EDDA*, to the story by the Danish scholar SAXO GRAMMATICUS and the poem by the English poet Matthew Arnold ("Balder Dead"). Many scholars think that the portrayal of the beautiful, good, passive god Balder was influenced by early Christian views of Jesus Christ.

**Balder's Dreams** When Balder became a young man, he began to have fearful dreams that seemed to foretell his death. None of the gods could understand the meaning of these dreams. His unhappiness cast sadness over all who lived in ASGARD, the home of the AESIR gods.

**Odin's Visit to the Volva** Odin, determined to solve the mystery of his son's dreams, mounted his horse, SLEIPNIR, and made the long journey to the underworld, NIFLHEIM. There he called up a seeress, one of the VOLVA. When she arose from her tomb, Odin introduced himself as VEGTAM, the Wanderer, son of Valtam.

Odin asked the Volva why the halls of HEL were decked with gold and the tables set for a grisly feast. The seeress replied that it was for Balder.

Odin asked who would slay Balder. The seeress answered that the blind HODUR would cast a fatal branch at his brother.

Odin then asked who would avenge Balder's death. The seeress answered that Odin would take RINDA as a wife, and their son would be VALI (2), who would take vengeance when he was only one night old.

Odin asked who would refuse to weep for Balder. At this question, which revealed that Vegtam knew or guessed more of the future than an ordinary mortal could, the Volva realized that Vegtam was in fact Odin, ALFODR.

She refused to answer any more questions and sank into her tomb, vowing to speak no more until LOKI's chains were unbound—that is, until the end of the world.

**Frigg and the Mistletoe** When Frigg realized that her son Balder's life was in danger, she sent her messengers to every corner of the world to extract promises not to harm her beloved son. Stones and metals, water and wind, fish and birds, reptiles and mammals, trees and flowers, insects, spiders, and scorpions, all creatures alive and all objects large and small swore that they would not harm Balder. Only one small green plant, the MISTLETOE, which grew on the mighty OAK tree, was not asked to make the promise, for it was so frail that no one paid attention to it.

**The Gods at Play** Word soon spread through Asgard that Balder was absolutely invulnerable: Nothing could harm him. The young gods, always ready for fun, made a game out of throwing things at Balder: stones, knives, sticks. Whatever they threw glanced off Balder's body, leaving him totally unharmed, to the merriment of all.

Only Loki did not join in the fun. Instead he disguised himself as an old crone and paid a visit to Frigg. Pretending to be astonished and disgusted at the sport the gods were making of Balder, Loki cunningly tricked Frigg into revealing the information he sought: that there was indeed one object in the world that had not taken the vow to be harmless to Balder. That object was the mistletoe that grew on the branches of the oak tree outside VALHALLA.

Loki hurried away, plucked a sprig of mistletoe, and hastened to the field of IDAVOLL, where the merry young gods were still at play. Only the blind god, Hodur, hung back, for he could not see.

Loki approached Hodur, put the mistletoe branch into his hands and offered to guide his aim. Hodur gladly accepted.

**The Death of Balder**  Hodur threw the fatal weapon and killed Balder. When Balder fell dead a terrible silence fell upon the gods, and then they cried out in a fearful wail. Balder, the good, the beautiful, the god of light, had been snuffed out like a bright candle. The gods would willingly have killed Hodur there and then, but ancient laws forbade that blood should be shed in Idavoll, so Hodur slunk off, alone and weeping.

**Balder's Funeral Pyre**  The gods built a huge funeral pyre on HRINGHORNI, Balder's dragon ship.

On it they laid the body, surrounding it with rich tapestries, heaps of flowers, vessels of food, clothes, weapons and precious jewels, as was the custom of the Norse.

NANNA, Balder's loving wife, fell grief-stricken over the body and died, so the gods placed her tenderly on the pyre beside her husband. Then they slew Balder's horse and hounds and placed them beside their master so that he should lack for nothing.

One by one all the gods drew near to say farewell to their beloved companion. Last of all came Odin, who took off his magic arm ring and placed it on his son's body. Then he stooped and put his mouth to Balder's ear, but nobody knew what he had whispered.

Balder, the shining god, is slain by Hodur, with the help of Loki and a sprig of mistletoe. *(Historical Picture Service–Chicago)*

When the gods tried to launch the ship, it was so heavy that not even THOR's phenomenal strength could move it. The gods accepted the help of HYROKKIN, a giantess who galloped onto the scene riding a huge wolf and holding reins of writhing snakes. Hyrokkin gave the vessel a mighty shove and launched it into the sea.

The funeral pyre burst into flames, and Thor went on board to consecrate the fire with his magic hammer, MJOLLNIR. As he was performing the rite, the dwarf LIT got under his feet, and Thor kicked him into the flames, where he burned to ashes along with Balder and Nanna.

The ship drifted out to sea, burning brightly, and the gods watched it in mourning until it disappeared and the world became dark.

**Hermod's Journey** When she had recovered sufficiently to speak, Frigg asked that one of the gods visit Hel in Niflheim and beg her to send Balder back from the land of the dead. Gallant HERMOD, another of Odin's sons, immediately volunteered to make the dreaded journey. Odin lent him his horse, Sleipnir, and for the second time the brave horse made the journey to the underworld. After traveling for nine days and nine nights and crossing many rivers, Hermod came to a stream, GIOLL. Sleipnir's hooves made the bridge over Gioll's stream shudder, and the sentry, MODGUD, challenged the rider. Upon learning that Balder was indeed in Niflheim, Hermod and Sleipnir made a great leap over the gate of Hel and landed safely on the other side. Balder could not leave the land of the dead without Hel's permission, and Hel refused to let him go unless all the world should rain tears for him. Hermod spent many hours with Balder and his wife, Nanna. They gave him gifts, including Odin's magic arm ring, DRAUPNIR, to take back to Asgard.

Then Hermod left to tell the gods his news. Surely the whole world would willingly weep to set Balder free.

**Thokk** When Hermod returned from the underworld with the news about Hel's condition for the return of Balder, messengers at once set out for every corner of the earth. Soon every god and goddess, every man and woman, every plant and every animal on land and sea and air, and every stone and metal was shedding tears for Balder.

In a dark cave sat an old woman, the giantess THOKK. She alone remained dry-eyed and hard of heart. "Balder never did anything for me," she said grimly. "Let Hel keep what is her due, for I have no tears for Balder." The messengers returned to Odin and Frigg with heavy hearts, and the gods mourned once more, for they knew now that Balder would never return to them.

**Vali Kills Hodur** Vali, Odin's youngest son, appeared in Asgard on the day of his birth, miraculously grown to full stature and carrying a quiver of arrows. He shot one of these at Hodur, who died. Thus the Norsemen's code of a death for a death was satisfied, and the Volva's prophecy was fulfilled.

**Ragnarok** At RAGNAROK, the time of the Regeneration, Balder came back from the dead, leading his blind brother, Hodur. All the survivors returned to Idavoll, where they created a new world.

**BARLEY** One of the oldest of cultivated cereal grasses, barley is widely distributed throughout the world. In northern lands it was used to make a malt brew and was a symbol of spring growth. FREY and GERDA are married in the barley patch named BARRI.

**BARRI (BARRE)** The sacred grove where the god FREY and the JOTUN maid GERDA were united. The name derives from BARLEY.

**BAUGI (Ring-Shaped)** A giant, the brother of SUTTUNG. Baugi employed ODIN, who was disguised as a worker, BOLVERK. Bolverk worked so well that Baugi agreed to lead him to the mountain where the MEAD of poetry was hidden, guarded by GUNLOD, Suttung's daughter. Baugi drilled a hole in the mountain with his augur, and Odin changed into a serpent and slithered through the hole to find Gunlod and the mead.

**BELI** The JOTUN brother of GERDA, FREY's beloved. Beli challenged Frey, and Frey killed him with a stag horn, as he had given away his magic sword as BRIDE PRICE to GYMIR, Gerda's father.

**BERGELMIR** Son of the HRIMTHURSSAR (frost giant) Thrudgelmir and grandson of YMIR, the primeval giant who appeared at the CREATION.

Bergelmir and his wife were the only surviving GIANTS after Ymir's death and the flood. They rode the flood on a hollowed-out tree trunk, the first boat. Because of them, the race of frost giants and ogres was able to survive in JOTUNHEIM.

**BERLING** One of the four DWARFS who made the BRISINGAMEN for the goddess FREYA. The others were ALFRIGG, DVALIN, and GRERR.

**BERSERKERS** Savage, reckless, furious warriors of an elite corps who fought for ODIN wearing only bear or wolf skins and no armor. In the sagas they were named after Berserk, a Norse hero of the eighth century who went into battle with his 12 sons.

In modern English usage, to *go berserk* means to "go into a frenzy."

**BESTLA** The giantess wife of BOR and mother of three gods, ODIN, VILI, and VE. She was the daughter of the giant BOLTHUR. Bestla appears in SNORRI STURLUSON's *PROSE EDDA*.

**BEYLA** The wife of BYGGVIR. Both were servants of the god FREY who attended a feast given by AEGIR (see "Loki's Mocking," under LOKI).

**BIFROST** (Trembling Path) The flaming, three-strand bridge between ASGARD and MIDGARD, also called the RAINBOW BRIDGE. Humans see the bridge as a rainbow spanning the distance between heaven and Earth.

The AESIR gods skillfully built Bifrost out of fire, air, and water, the three materials that can be seen as the colors of the rainbow: red (fire), blue (air), and green (water). Though it looked fragile, Bifrost was immensely strong.

The gods appointed HEIMDALL to be the watchman of the bridge, for his senses were keen and he had a marvelous horn, GIALAR, whose blast would ring throughout NINE WORLDS if the HRIMTHURSSAR set foot on Bifrost.

The Aesir gods crossed Bifrost regularly to go to council meetings at URDARBRUNN, a sacred place. Only THOR, the thunder god, could not walk or ride across Bifrost, lest the heat of his lightning harmed the bridge.

At RAGNAROK, the end of the world, Bifrost would shatter under the terrible weight of the MUSPELL and frost giants who came to fight the gods on VIGRID, the vast battlefield.

**BIL AND YUKI** (BIL AND HJUKI; the Waxing and Waning Moon) The two earth children stolen by MANI, the man of the Moon, to help him drive his chariot across the skies. They were the children of VIDFINN, who had sent them to fetch water from the spring BYRGIR in a pail carried between them on a pole. Legend has it that the shadows we see on the Moon are those of the two children carrying their pail of water.

A 19th-century Englishman, the Reverend S. Baring-Gould, in *Curious Myths of the Middle Ages* (1866) claimed that the popular nursery rhyme about Jack and Jill, who "went up the hill to fetch a pail of water" had its origin in the ancient tale of Bil and Yuki.

(See also "Sun and Moon," under CREATION.)

**BILLING** In some tellings of the myths Billing is king of the Ruthenians (Russians) and the father of RINDA, who was to be wooed by ODIN (see "Vali, the Avenger," under VALI [2]).

**BILSKIRNIR** (Lightning) THOR's dwelling in ASGARD. As befitted the god's large size and his fondness for giving huge banquets, Bilskirnir, with 540 rooms, was the largest hall in all Asgard.

**BLODIGHOFI** (Bloodyhoof) The god FREY's magical horse that could leap through flames unharmed.

**BOAR** A male swine or pig. People have admired the boar since ancient times for its courage. It has been hunted and killed for its succulent flesh, tough bristles, sturdy hide, and sharp tusks; in fact, no part of this creature goes unused by humankind.

In Norse mythology and history FREY's golden boar was named GULLINBURSTI (Golden Bristles). Gullinbursti's image is found on many helmets and shields worn by ancient warriors as a symbol of good luck in battle. In the winter months a sacrificial boar was offered up to the god Frey. The pagan custom is still remembered in many countries at Yuletide or

Christmas (see also "The Mead of Poetry," under ODIN), where roast pig, pork, or ham may be the festive dish. In Sweden Yuletide cakes are baked in the shape of a boar. In England many inns are called The Boar's Head in recognition of the ancient custom of serving a boar's head at Christmas.

Also mentioned in Norse mythology is the golden boar HILDISVINI, belonging to Frey's sister, FREYA, and the boar SAEHRIMNIR, who was nightly sacrificed at ODIN's VALHALLA for the feasting of the heroes. Saehrimnir came back to life each day.

**BODN** (Vessel)    A jar, one of three containers in which the blood of KVASIR was kept (see also "The Mead of Poetry," under ODIN). The other two were called ODRORIR and SON.

**BOLTHUR** (BOLTHORN, BOLTURON; Thorn of Evil)    The JOTUN father of BESTLA and a son whose name is unknown. Bestla married BOR and bore him three sons, ODIN, VILI, and VE. Thus Bolthur was Odin's grandfather.

When Odin hanged himself from the World Tree, YGGDRASIL, to gain wisdom, he learned nine songs from the son of Bolthor, Odin's uncle (see "Lord of the Gallows," under ODIN). In Norse mythology and folklore there was often a close bond between a man and his maternal uncle, who sometimes acted as godfather or surrogate father.

**BOLVERK** (Evil-Doer)    The name ODIN used when he went to JOTUNHEIM to steal back the MEAD of poetry. Odin took the form of a tall, strong man. When he found nine slaves working wearily in a field, he offered to sharpen their scythes with his whetstone. The slaves were so impressed with the sharpness of their blades after Bolverk had honed them that they asked for the whetstone. Odin-Bolverk threw it up in the air. As they scrambled to catch it, the nine workers managed to kill each other with their scythes. Thus Odin-Bolverk was able to ingratiate himself with their master, BAUGI, who now had no workers and was glad to employ the stranger. As a reward for his work, Baugi eventually led Odin to the cave where the MEAD of poetry was hidden. The character of Bolverk shows Odin as a devious, cruel being who will shed the blood of others to gain his ends.

**BOR** (BUR)    Son of BURI, who was known as the father of the gods. According to early Norse poetry, Bor married BESTLA, the daughter of a GIANT. Bor's sons killed the first giant, YMIR, and created the world from his body parts. According to SNORRI STURLUSON, Bor's sons were ODIN, VILI, and VE.

**BRAGI**    The god of poetry, eloquence, and music. Bragi was the son of ODIN and GUNLOD and husband of IDUNN. Bragi does not play a major role in Norse myths. He is pictured as playing on a harp and singing so sweetly that even the trees and flowers are charmed by him. Norsemen called their poets or skalds *bragamen* or *bragawomen*. In English the verb to *brag* means "to boast rather loudly of one's achievements." Because Odin had a great knowledge of poetry, some scholars see Bragi as another facet of Odin's personality.

**BREIDABLIK** (Broad Gleaming)    The shining hall of the god BALDER in ASGARD.

**BRIDE PRICE**    In ancient times, and still among some peoples, the money or goods (dowry) given to the family of the bride by the bridegroom or his family. In the story "Frey and Gerda," FREY's magic sword was the bride price for Gerda. In another Norse story the giant THRYM offers THOR's stolen hammer in return for FREYA as his bride.

**BRISINGAMEN** (Brisings' Necklace)    The golden necklace given to the goddess FREYA by the four DWARFS ALFRIGG, BERLING, DVALIN, and GRERR. It is not known who the Brisings were. Freya was the goddess of fertility; a necklace is often used as a fertility symbol. Freya lends the necklace to the god THOR in "The Theft of Thor's Hammer."

**BROKK**    A DWARF. SNORRI STURLUSON tells the story of how the trickster god LOKI bet Brokk and his brother, EITRI, that they could not make gifts for the gods as wonderful as those that other dwarfs had already made. Brokk accepted the bet and set out with his brother to make a BOAR with golden bristles, a gold ring, and THOR's hammer. Brokk worked the bellows to blow air on the smith's fire, and Eitri crafted the objects. Loki, meanwhile, pestered Brokk. As Eitri worked on Thor's hammer, the last of the three objects, Loki turned himself into a fly and bit Brokk's eyelid, causing it to bleed into the dwarf's eye. As a result Brokk stopped working the bellows and the fire cooled. It was for this reason that Thor's famous hammer, MJOLLNIR, had a short handle. Despite Loki's interference Brokk and Eitri won the bet. This story survives only in Snorri's work.

See also TREASURES OF THE DWARFS.

**BURI** Ancestor of the gods. Buri appeared at the time of the CREATION, when the cosmic cow AUDHUMLA brought him to life from under the primeval ice. In time Buri had a son named BOR who married the giantess BESTLA and became the father of the gods ODIN, VILI, and VE.

**BYGGVIR** One of the god FREY'S servants. Byggvir is married to BEYLA. The couple served at the feast that AEGIR gave to the gods (see "Loki's Mocking," under LOKI).

**BYRGIR** The well to which the earth children, BIL AND YUKI, had gone to fetch water before being stolen away by MANI, the man of the Moon.

**CAT** In world mythology the domestic cat is often venerated or feared as a witch in disguise or as a witch's "creature." In Norse mythology the goddess FREYA, who had magic powers, had a chariot drawn by two gray or black cats.

**CAULDRON** A large pot or kettle used for boiling. In "Thor and Hymir Go Fishing," THOR goes in search of HYMIR's huge cauldron because the gods need it for brewing ale. Later, in "Loki's Mocking," (see under LOKI), the sea god AEGIR gives a banquet for the gods. He brews the ale in the cauldron that Thor and TYR took from Hymir. The cauldron features in many medieval tales, especially those where witches brew magic broths.

**CODEX REGIUS** A manuscript found in the 17th century in a farmhouse in Iceland and presented by Bishop Brynjólfur Sveinsson to the king of Denmark, where it was part of the royal collection for several centuries. About one-half of this collection is the poems that make up the *POETIC EDDA*, a primary source of stories and information on Norse mythology. The manuscript was preserved in the Royal Library in Copenhagen, Denmark, and is now preserved in Iceland.

**COW** This female mammal is noted for the nurturing properties of her milk. In many world mythologies she is the symbol of the Great Mother and of CREATION. In the *PROSE EDDA* and the *POETIC EDDA* of the Norse, the cow is AUDHUMLA.

**CREATION** The mythology of each people has its own story of how the world was created. In Norse mythology, at the beginning there was a swirling chaos of mists and fog, freezing cold, howling winds, and terrifying fire.

The following story of the Creation is from SNORRI STURLUSON's *PROSE EDDA*, his major sources being *VOLUSPA*, *GRIMNISMAL*, and *VAFTHRUDNISMAL*.

**The Chasm** There was no Sun, no Moon, no stars, no land or sea. There was only a yawning chasm called GINNUNGAGAP.

To the north of Ginnungagap was NIFLHEIM, land of cold mists; to the south was MUSPELLHEIM, the land of fire. From Niflheim's spring, HVERGELMIR, flowed the 11 poisonous rivers of the ELIVAGAR. They emptied into the chasm, froze, and filled it with venomous ice. From Muspellheim came sheets of fire that turned the ice into mists and dense fog.

For millions of years fire and ice interacted with each other until at last there came sparks of life. The first life took the form of a huge, giant, YMIR, and a gigantic cow, AUDHUMLA, that nourished Ymir with her milk. She in turn licked the salty stones around Ginnungagap for nourishment.

As Audhumla licked at the icy, salty stones around Ginnungagap, she uncovered the hairs of a man's head. Soon she uncovered the entire head and finally the whole body of a handsome, humanlike creature. He was BURI, the ancestor of the gods.

Buri produced a son named BOR, who married a giantess, BESTLA, who gave him three sons, ODIN, VILI, and VE, the first gods.

Meanwhile, as Ymir slept, hordes of hideous giant children sprouted from his body. They were the HRIMTHURSSAR and JOTUNS.

Odin and his brothers, the sons of Bor, quarreled with the unruly gang of giants. Finally they attacked and killed Ymir, the father of them all. Immense floods of blood spurted from the fallen giant and drowned all the frost giants except BERGELMIR and his wife, who rode out the flood on a hollowed tree trunk, the first boat.

Odin, Vili, and Ve dragged Ymir's huge body to Ginnungagap, and there they set about creating the world. They made the earth from his flesh, mountains and hills from his bones, and rocks and boulders from his teeth. His curly hair became leafy trees and all vegetation. The lakes and seas and oceans were made from his blood.

**Sky**   Then they made the sky's dome from Ymir's skull and flung his brains aloft to make the clouds. Snorri says the four DWARFS NORDI, SUDRI, AUSTRI, and VESTRI held up the four corners of the sky. The four points of the compass, North, South, East, and West, are named after these dwarfs. The gods took sparks and embers from Muspellheim's fires and made the Sun, Moon, and stars.

**Jotunheim**   The sons of Bor gave the new generation of giants, the race founded by Bergelmir, the land named JOTUNHEIM. They bade the giants stay there.

**Midgard**   Then they put Ymir's eyebrows around a green piece of land, forming a pleasant enclosure they called MIDGARD, or Middle Earth.

**Night and Day**   Once the gods had created the world and placed the Sun and Moon in the sky, they made night and day.

NOTT (Night) was a beautiful giantess with a dark complexion and hair of midnight black. She was the daughter of NARFI, one of the first giants. She married three times. Her first husband was NAGLFARI, father of AUD. Her second was ANNAR, father of FJORGYN (1). With her third husband, DELLING, she had a fair son named DAG (Day).

The gods sent Nott and Dag up into the heavens in horse-drawn chariots to ride around the world. They created darkness and light, as one followed the other through the skies.

Nott drove first, with her lead horse, HRIMFAXI. The froth from his bit fell to Earth as dewdrops.

After Nott came Dag with his horse, SKINFAXI. His golden glow lit up the heavens and the Earth.

**Sun and Moon**   The gods placed the Sun and the Moon in chariots, drawn by splendid horses. The horses were driven by SOL and MANI, the daughter and the son of a man from Midgard whose name was MUNDILFARI.

Sol's horses were ARVAKR and ALSVID. A shield, SVALIN, in Sol's chariot protected her from the Sun, whose brilliant rays would have burned her to a cinder. Mani's horse was ALDSVIDER.

Mani, the man of the Moon, stole two earth children to help him drive his chariot. Their names were BIL AND YUKI.

SUN AND MOON could never pause in their journeys across the heavens, for they were forever pursued by the terrible wolves SKOLL and HATI. Each month Hati, it was said, took a bite out of the Moon and tried to gobble it up. But the Moon escaped and grew whole again. In the end the wolves will devour both Sun and Moon and cast the world into darkness at RAGNAROK.

**The First Humans**   The first man was ASK (Ash) and the first woman, EMBLA (Elm). The first three AESIR gods, Odin, Vili, and Ve, created them.

The gods were walking along the seashore when they saw two tree trunks lying at the edge of the water. The forms of the trees were beautiful. Odin breathed life into them. Vili gave them the ability to speak and think. Ve gave them warmth and color and movement.

The gods gave them Midgard in which to live. All human beings were descended from them. HEIMDALL later created the different social classes of men and women.

**The Dwarfs**   The gods made gnomes and dwarfs from the grubs in Ymir's rotting corpse. They gave them human form and endowed them with brains, but they were ugly, misshapen little creatures, greedy and selfish. The gods gave them SVARTALFHEIM, the dark realm underground, and put them in charge of the earth's treasures of gold, other precious metals, and gems. The dwarfs were master smiths.

See also TREASURES OF THE DWARFS.

**Asgard**   The gods created for themselves the beautiful realm of ASGARD, home of the Aesir gods. It was linked to Midgard by BIFROST, the RAINBOW BRIDGE, and it was sheltered by the great World Tree, YGGDRASIL, which touched all the worlds.

# D

**DAG** (Day)   The son of NOTT and her third husband, DELLING. ODIN set Nott and Dag in the sky to ride around the world, bringing darkness and light at regular intervals. Dag's horse was SKINFAXI (Shining Mane) whose golden glow lit up the Earth.

See also "Night and Day," under CREATION.

**DAIN (1)**   A DWARF mentioned only in *HYND-LULJOTH*, a part of the *POETIC EDDA*, as one of the creators of the gold-bristled boar HILDISVINI. According to this poem Dain and his brother, NABBI, made the magical boar.

**DAIN (2)** (Dead)   An elf, perhaps a DWARF, who was talented at writing and reading RUNES.

**DAIN (3)**   A fully grown male deer, or stag, that lived among the branches of YGGDRASIL, the World Tree, and ate its leaves.

**DAINSLEIF** (Dain's Heirloom)   A sword made by the DWARF DAIN (1), according to SNORRI STURLUSON. This sword was cursed: Once drawn, it must kill a man before it could be returned to the sheath. A blow from this magical sword never failed to kill or cause a wound that never healed. To rescue his daughter Hild, the legendary warrior and king Hogni drew Dainsleif to kill her abductor, Hedin Hjarrandason.

**DELLING** (Dawn, Dayspring)   The third husband of NOTT. Their son was called DAG. Delling was related to the sons of Bor, the gods ODIN, VILI, and VE.

See also "Night and Day," under CREATION.

**DENMARK**   A nation in northwestern Europe consisting of the Jutland peninsula and many nearby islands in the Baltic Sea. Denmark is part of SCANDINAVIA and shares a common history with NORWAY, SWEDEN, and ICELAND. They are all home to NORSE mythology. The VIKINGS are the ancestors of the people in these modern-day nations.

According to a story by SNORRI STURLUSON, the goddess GEFION plowed the island for Zealand (Sjaelland in Danish) from the mainland of Sweden, using the strength of her four sons, who were giant oxen. Important archaeological finds concerning Norse myths have come from this country; Zealand, for example, has an important collection of rock carvings from the late Bronze Age, which began around 1000 B.C., that portray religious scenes. Two elaborately carved little wagons, which would have carried the gods, came from a site near Dejberg on the Jutland peninsula. Also a tree coffin, where the trunk was carved out to make room for the body, was found near Egtved. The National Museum of Denmark houses many Norse artifacts.

**DISIR**   Female guardian spirits associated with death. The Disir (singular, Dis) watched over individuals, families, and perhaps entire neighborhoods. Some experts believe the Disir were malicious, harmful spirits, who sought bad things for the people they watched over; however, other experts suggest that the NORSE people also believed in a positive influence of the Disir in a person's life and that a Dis brought good to a home and its family. The goddess FREYA was also referred to as Vanadis, which means the "Dis of the VANIR."

This type of spirit is mentioned in the Eddic poem GRIMNISMAL, and the Disir play an important role in the *Saga of Tryggvason*. More information about them survives in place-names in SCANDINAVIA and in histories written in later centuries.

**DIVINATION** The act or practice of predicting the future, particularly through a ritual or ceremony. The ancient NORSE people held strong beliefs in the ability of some people, animals, and objects to predict the future. They sought omens and warnings from sacred horses, performed ceremonies full of chants and singing and led by a seeress to learn what would happen in battle, and studied the arrangement of twigs to learn of their fates. Divination was closely connected with the magical art form known as SEID.

**DRAGON** A mythical beast, usually represented as a large, winged, fire-breathing reptile similar to a crocodile or a SERPENT. In Norse myth the dragon NITHOG feeds on the root of the World Tree, YGGDRASIL. In Norse and Germanic legend, from which Norse mythology evolved, the dragon FAFNIR guards his ill-gotten treasure and is eventually slain by the young hero SIGURD.

**DRAUPNIR** (Dropper) The golden ring or arm ring made for the great god ODIN by the dwarfs EITRI and BROKK (see TREASURES OF THE DWARFS). Every ninth night, eight other rings dropped from Draupnir, each as heavy and bright as the first.

In the story "Frey and Gerda" (see under FREY), Gerda was not tempted by the ring. In "Balder's Funeral" (see under BALDER), Odin placed Draupnir on the funeral pyre; it was then returned to him by HERMOD, the messenger god who had gone to the underworld to try to bring Balder back to the living.

**DROMI** The second of three chains with which the gods tried to bind the dangerous wolf FENRIR. Though stronger than the first chain (LAEDING), this ordinary metal chain could not hold tight the powerful and evil wolf. Only the magical third chain, GLEIPNER, successfully secured Fenrir until the time of RAGNAROK, the conflict that brought an end to the world of the gods.

**DVALIN** The DWARF who with his three brothers, ALFRIGG, BERLING, and GRERR, fashioned the golden BRISINGAMEN coveted by the goddess FREYA. The other three dwarfs are never heard of again, but the story of ALVIS makes reference to Dvalin, who was turned to stone by the rising Sun.

See also DVALIN'S DELIGHT.

**DVALIN'S DELIGHT** The ironic name given by the DWARFS to the Sun. Dwarfs, gnomes, trolls, and other denizens of underground caves are terrified of the Sun, for it turns them to stone. They must never be caught aboveground in daylight.

See also ALVIS.

**DWARFS** The small, misshapen creatures made at the CREATION from the grubs in the giant YMIR's dead body. They were given the realm of SVARTALFHEIM (land of the dark ELVES) in which to live. The gods put them in charge of Earth's underground treasures: precious metals and gems. They were master craftsmen and fashioned many treasures for the gods (see *TREASURES OF THE DWARFS*).

SNORRI STURLUSON lists dozens of names of dwarfs, but few of them are ever heard of again in the surviving records of Norse myths. Among the more memorable ones are

- ALVIS, who like many of the dwarfs had a vast store of knowledge and poetically listed the various names for the 13 most important words in medieval Scandinavian vocabulary
- BROKK and EITRI, who fashioned various gifts for the gods
- DVALIN, one of the dwarfs who made the BRISINGAMEN coveted by the goddess FREYA and who was turned into stone at sunrise
- ANDVARI, the dwarf who was tricked by LOKI into giving up his gold hoard upon

Deep under the earth, dwarfs crafted metals and gems into treasures for the gods and goddesses. *(Historical Picture Service–Chicago)*

which he then placed a curse (see "Otr's Ransom," under OTR)

- LIT, the dwarf who was inadvertently cremated on BALDER's funeral pyre

- NORDI, SUDRI, AUSTRI, and VESTRI, the four dwarfs who were bidden to hold up the four corners of the sky

# E

**EAGLE**  A symbol of strength and death in Norse mythology. The eagle was also an image of the battle-field, for it often ate at the dead bodies.

An eagle was one of the three birds of ODIN—the other two were RAVENs—who was the god of death, among other things. Odin is often pictured with an eagle. He occasionally took on the form of an eagle, as did other gods and GIANTs. An eagle also sat on the topmost branches of YGGDRASIL, the World Tree, where it flapped its wings and created the winds in MIDGARD, the world of HUMANS.

Many images of the eagle appear in stone carvings dating from the era of the Norse gods and found in SCANDINAVIA. They also appear frequently on helmets and small brooches. The eagle's curved beak distinguishes this bird from ravens, which have straight beaks.

**EARTH**  In Old NORSE, both Jord and FJORGYN (1) mean "earth." Both are names of mythological beings and are used at times to refer to the land or the soil. Jord is the most frequent name used for the giantess who was the mother of THOR, son of ODIN; in this role she is sometimes known as Fjorgyn. Jord is also found in SKALDIC POETRY as a name for the celestial body Earth.

**EARTH MOTHER**  (Earth Goddess)  A general name for a female spirit or deity worshiped by peoples all over the world. Believers prayed to her for fine weather and good crops, for food and shelter, and for numerous sons and daughters. In Norse mythology the first Earth goddesses had no distinct form but later were identified with FJORGYN (1), FRIGG, and FREYA.

**EDDAS, THE**  Two distinct works: the *POETIC EDDA*, also called the *Elder Edda*, and the *PROSE EDDA*, sometimes known as the *Snorra Edda* or *Younger Edda*. The *Eddas* are the main source of knowledge about Norse mythology.

The *Poetic Edda* is a collection of poems on mythological and legendary themes, written down at different times and by different poets between the eighth and 13th centuries. They were discovered in 1643 by the Icelandic bishop Brynjólfur Sveinsson. (The *Poetic Edda* was sometimes called *Saemund's Edda* in the mistaken belief that it had been written by the medieval bishop SAEMUND SIGFÚSSON.)

The *Prose Edda*, "younger" because it was not put to paper until around 1220, was written by Icelandic poet, historian, and diplomat SNORRI STURLUSON. It is a handbook of Norse mythology, designed as a guide for poets to encourage them to write in the style of the ancient poets of the Viking age.

These two great books helped keep alive the memory of the ancient gods and their exploits, which otherwise might have been lost forever with the coming of Christianity to the northern lands.

**EGGTHER**  Watchman of the giants. At RAGNAROK, the end of the world, he sat upon a grave mound and grimly played his harp.

**EGIL**  Two characters with this name appear in Norse mythology. The existing documents leave it unclear whether each use of the name referred to one figure or to different people. Egil, apparently, was a common name in the folklore of SCANDINAVIA.

One person named Egil was a servant of THOR, according to SNORRI STURLUSON. He guarded Thor's goats while the god was visiting the giant HYMIR. This Egil may have been the father of Thor's human servants THIALFI and ROSKVA.

Another Egil is the subject of a popular Icelandic SAGA, or epic story, known today as *Egil's Saga*. He was a very skilled and talented archer, and the brother of Weland, the blacksmith.

**EIKTHYRNIR** (Oak Thorny)  The fully grown male deer, or stag, that stood on the roof of VALHALLA, ODIN's famous palace, and nibbled at the leaves of the great oak tree LAERAD, around which the hall had been built. Drops of an unnamed fluid dripped from Eikthyrnir's antlers, and from it came all of the great rivers of the world. Besides being named in Norse manuscripts, Eikthyrnir is portrayed on a 10th-century carved stone cross from Cumbria, England.

**EINHERJAR** (Lone Fighters)  The fallen HUMAN warriors chosen by ODIN to live and revel with him in VALHALLA until the end of time, known as RAGNAROK. These special warriors are described in many written sources from ICELAND. Older poems and stories describe them as special warriors of Odin who are served by the VALKYRIES. In other works, including the *PROSE EDDA* written by SNORRI STURLUSON, the Einherjar are dead warriors who go to live in Valhalla with Odin. There they feast each day on the meat of the magical boar SAEHRIMNIR and practice their warfare in preparation for Ragnarok, the final conflict between the gods and the giants.

Scholars suggest that the image of the Einherjar is based on a very ancient cult that worshiped Odin, the god of the dead and of battle. Many kings and princes of SCANDINAVIA were followers of this cult and dedicated themselves and the people they killed in battle to Odin.

**EIR**  A goddess and healer or physician. Little is now known of Eir. She appears in the works of SNORRI STURLUSON and is mentioned once in the older *POETIC EDDA*. Eir is one of the 12 or 13 highest-ranking goddesses, according to Snorri's list of deities. She is also one of the handmaids of the beautiful giantess MENGLOD.

Eir means "peace," "mercy," or "clemency," traits some see as important to her role as a physician. That Snorri and others even named this goddess suggests to

scholars that Eir once played an important role in Norse religion.

**EITRI**  A dwarf who helped create three of the precious objects of the gods. In a competition, the trickster god LOKI bet the dwarf BROKK and his brother, Eitri, that they could not make anything as fine as the gifts another group of dwarfs had already made for the gods—a golden headpiece, a ship, and a spear. With Brokk at the bellows Eitri successfully crafted a boar with golden bristles, GULLINBURSTI; a gold ring, DRAUPNIR; and THOR's hammer, MJOLLNIR.

Experts working in the later part of the 20th century agree that earlier scholars had mistakenly applied the name Sindri to the brother of Brokk, Eitri.

See also *TREASURES OF THE DWARFS*.

**ELDER EDDA**  See *POETIC EDDA*.

**ELDHRIMNIR** (Soot-Blackened)  The name of the cauldron at VALHALLA in which the magic boar, SAEHRIMNIR, was cooked every night for the feasting of the gods and heroes.

**ELDIR** (Man of Fire)  One of the two servants of the ancient sea god AEGIR. Eldir was on duty as the gatekeeper, or outer guard, to Aegir's castle when LOKI tried to return to the banquet where he had killed Aegir's other servant, FIMAFENG. Eldir challenged Loki, the trickster god, by making him feel guilty for his acts, but Loki convinced Eldir to allow him back into the castle.

**ELIVAGAR**  The collective name for 11 venomous rivers that surged from the spring HVERGELMIR in the underworld, NIFLHEIM. The rivers had fearsome NAMES that related to howling and boiling and storming: Fimbulthul, Fjorm, Gjoll, Gunnthra, Hrid, Leipt, Slid, Syol, Sylg, Vid, and Ylg. The rivers froze and roared into GINNUNGAGAP, the abyss, as glaciers. The first giant, YMIR, was formed from the frozen poison of the Elivagar (see CREATION).

In the story "Thor's Duel with Hrungnir," THOR tells of carrying AURVANDIL in a basket across the Elivagar. In the story "Thor and Hymir Go Fishing," Thor and TYR journey to the east of the Elivagar in Thor's GOAT chariot.

**ELJUDNIR** (ELVIDNIR; Damp with Sleet)   The hall of the goddess HEL in her realm, NIFLHEIM, the underworld. Eljudnir was a great home with very high walls, high banisters, and huge gates. Her maidservant in this palace was GANGLOT, and GANGLATI was her manservant. Some sources say that it was in Eljudnir that Hel met with the god HERMOD when he traveled to the underworld to rescue the spirit of the god BALDER.

**ELLI** (ELLE)   Old age in the form of an old woman whom the god THOR wrestled at UTGARD-LOKI's hall. Thor was, of course, defeated, for no one can win against old age.

**ELVES**   In Norse mythology elves do not play an active part; they are mentioned only in passing. For example, the Vanir god FREY was sometimes called Lord of the Elves. The domain of the elves was Alfheim. When the dwarf ALVIS cited the 13 most important words in the language, he mentioned the elves only twice. In some accounts of BALDER's funeral the elves came to mourn, along with the gods, giants, and dwarfs. The Dark Elves, whose domain was SVARTALFHEIM, seem to be indistinguishible from DWARFS.

**EMBLA**   The first woman, who was created from an alder or elm tree by the first three AESIR gods, ODIN, VILI, and VE (see "The First Humans," under CREATION). In Norse myth, all HUMANS were descended from Embla and ASK, the first man.

# F

**FAFNIR** Son of the magician HREIDMAR and brother of REGIN and OTR. Fafnir killed his father for his hoard of gold, then turned himself into a dragon to guard the gold. He was himself killed by the hero SIGURD.

**FALCON** A bird of prey that hunts during the day. Like its relatives the hawk and the EAGLE, the falcon has extraordinary eyesight and powers of flight. In Norse mythology the goddess FREYA possessed a suit of falcon feathers that enabled her to travel wherever she wanted.

Freya lent her suit of feathers to LOKI so that he might rescue IDUNN and again so that he might find MJOLLNIR, the hammer (see "The Theft of Thor's Hammer," under THOR). On another occasion, in "Thor and the Giant Geirrod," Loki borrowed a falcon suit from FRIGG, the wife of ODIN.

**FARBAUTI** (Cruel Striker) A giant, or JOTUN, the father of the trickster god, LOKI. Loki's mother was the giantess LAUFEY, according to SNORRI STURLUSON. Some say that Farbauti struck Laufey with a bolt of lightning, after which she gave birth to Loki.

**FENRIR** (FENRIS) The WOLF who was the off-spring of the trickster god, LOKI, and the ogress ANGRBODA. He was the brother of HEL and of JOR-MUNGAND, the Midgard Serpent. Fenrir was so huge that when he opened his mouth, his jaws stretched from Earth to heaven. He was eventually bound by the gods and doomed to remain in chains until RAG-NAROK (the end of the world), when he would kill the great god ODIN. Fenrir in turn would die at the hand of VIDAR, one of Odin's sons. (SNORRI STURLU-SON's vivid version of this myth in the PROSE EDDA is the only surviving source.)

**Fenrir and the Gods** FENRIR was so huge and hairy that the AESIR, the gods of ASGARD, were frightened of him. Only TYR was brave enough to befriend the monster wolf and feed him. But as Fenrir grew bigger, the gods decided to protect themselves and chain him. One chain was called LAEDING, another, DROMI. Fenrir easily broke the chains. Then the gods sent SKIRNIR, the servant of the god FREY, to seek the help of the DWARFS, who lived in the earth.

The dwarfs fashioned a silken bond, called GLEIP-NIR, from

- the sound of a cat's paws
- the hairs of a maiden's beard
- the roots of a mountain
- the dreams of a bear
- the breath of a fish
- the spittle of a bird

Because none of these things seems to exist on Earth, no person or thing could break this bond.

The gods persuaded Fenrir to go with them to a lonely island, LYNGVI, in the middle of Lake AMSVARTNIR. They asked Fenrir if he would allow himself to be tied up once more and use his mighty strength to break the bond. He agreed to be bound if one of the gods would put a hand into Fenrir's mouth and guarantee that the wolf would be set free. Tyr, the most fair-minded of the gods, agreed to put his hand into Fenrir's mouth.

Once secured in Gleipner, Fenrir could not break the bond. He clamped down on Tyr's hand and bit it off. The gods attached Gleipnir to a heavy chain, GELGJA, and passed the chain through a hole into a large rock named GIOLL (1). Then the gods thrust a sword into the wolf's mouth so that it would remain wide open. There Fenrir remained bound

Fenrir, the monster wolf, bit off the hand of the god Tyr. *(New York Public Library Picture Collection)*

and gagged until the fatal day of Ragnarok, when Fenrir got his revenge and killed the chief god, ODIN.

For the Norsemen of Scandinavia the wolf was an ever-present danger.

**FENSALIR** (Water, Sea, or Bog Hall)   The palace or home of the goddess FRIGG, wife of ODIN and mother of BALDER. In this hall, the god LOKI tricked Frigg into revealing that her son's one vulnerability was MISTLETOE. Some experts suggest that Fensalir was located in a swamp or bog because followers of Frigg worshiped near a spring.

**FIMAFENG** (Swift)   One of the servants of AEGIR, the sea god. Fimafeng was stabbed to death by the trickster god, LOKI, at Aegir's banquet for the gods.

**FIMBULVETR** (Fimbul Winter, Mighty Winter) The winter of winters, the worst of all possible winters. The Fimbulvetr lasted for three years without respite and took place just before RAGNAROK, the end of the world. It brought terrible hardships, with driving snowstorms from all four points of the compass, vicious winds, bitter cold, and unyielding ice. People starved and lost all hope and goodness as they fought for their lives. They committed terrible crimes and started many wars.

**FJALAR (1)** (All-Knower)   The beautiful red rooster that crowed to the giants at the beginning of RAGNAROK, the end of the world.

**FJALAR (2)**   One of the wicked DWARFS (along with GALAR) who killed KVASIR, the wise man (see "The Mead of Poetry," under ODIN).

**FJOLSVID**   The giant who guarded the gate in JOTUNHEIM behind which the fair MENGLOD waited for her lover, SVIPDAG.

**FJORGYN (1)** (FJORGVIN; Earth)   One of two names (the other being Jord) for the giantess who was the mother of THOR, the thunder god and son of ODIN, the most powerful god. The word *fjorgyn* is also used in Norse mythology to refer to the "land" or "earth."

**FJORGYN (2)** (FJORGYNN)   The father of the goddess FRIGG, according to the works of Icelandic poet SNORRI STURLUSON. According to modern experts in the Old NORSE language, the similarity between the feminine form of this word, which was the name of a giantess (see FJORGYN [1]), and masculine form is a result of transliteration, the methods of using the alphabet of one language to replicate the sounds of another language. In Old Norse spelling, there are distinctions between the names for the mother of THOR and the father of Frigg that are not evident in modern English.

**FLOOD**   At the time of CREATION in Norse mythology, the giant YMIR was killed by the gods. His spurting blood created a flood. All the giants were drowned except BERGELMIR and his wife, who created a new race of giants. Oceans, seas, and lakes were formed from Ymir's blood. In the Old Testament Bible (Genesis), Noah and his family and pairs of animals are the only survivors of a flood. Stories of floods occur in many mythologies around the world, from India and Russia to New Guinea and North and South America.

**FOLKVANGER** (Field of Folk)   The part of ASGARD in which the hall of the goddess FREYA was situated. In the hall, SESSRUMNIR, she welcomed the slain heroes she shared with ODIN.

**FORNJOT** (Destroyer)   A giant. Thirteenth-century Icelandic author SNORRI STURLUSON identified Fornjot as the father of the wind. Modern scholars believe him to be a very old giant, perhaps one of the oldest figures in Norse mythology. Fornjot may also have been father of the HRIMTHURSSAR, or frost giants.

**FORSETI**   God of justice and conciliation. Forseti was the son of BALDER and NANNA. His hall was GLITNIR. Not much is known about Forseti, but place-names such as Forsetlund, near Oslo Fjord in Norway, suggest that he once may have been an important god.

**FREKI** (Ravenous)   One of the wolf companions of the god ODIN. The other was GERI, whose name also means "ravenous." Odin fed the wolves all the meat that was given to him, for he needed only to drink divine MEAD to survive. The wolves attended him at HLIDSKIALF, his high seat, and also at VALHALLA.

**FREY** (FREYR; Lord)   One of the great gods of the Norse. His name means "lord" (as his sister FREYA's means "lady"). Frey was the lord of the Sun, rain, and harvests. He was a shining god, bringing fertility and prosperity to all. Son of the VANIR god NIORD, Frey was one of the hostages asked to live in ASGARD after the *WAR BETWEEN THE AESIR AND THE VANIR*. His home was ALFHEIM (elfland), and he was sometimes known as Lord of the Elves.

Among the *TREASURES OF THE DWARFS* that went to Frey were the ship SKIDBLADNIR, which could carry all the gods and their horses and armor and yet be folded small enough to fit in a pouch; the golden boar GULLINBURSTI, which plowed the earth and made it green; and a magic sword that struck out at JOTUNS and trolls of its own accord. Frey gave this sword as a BRIDE PRICE to GERDA's father, GYMIR. He would regret its loss at RAGNAROK, when he battled with the fire demon SURT and lost his life.

Frey wed Gerda after his servant SKIRNIR had wooed her for him. Many scholars interpret the story "Frey and Gerda" as a legend about the wooing of the frozen Earth (Gerda) by the warm Sun (Frey).

Historically, the worship of Frey was widespread and persistent, especially among the people of SWE-DEN. Around the year 1200 there was a magnificent statue of Frey (called there Fricco, the Lover) alongside the two other great gods ODIN and THOR in Uppsala, Sweden.

**Frey and Gerda**   One myth has it that Frey dared to climb onto the Odin's high seat, HLIDSKIALF, where no one but the great god and sometimes his wife, FRIGG, were allowed to sit. From this vantage point Odin could see all the NINE WORLDS.

Frey looked about him, and his gaze was transfixed by a dazzling vision. He saw GERDA, the fair daughter of the giant Gymir. As she opened the gates to her palace, her shapely arms shone with such radiance that the Earth and the sky around her shimmered.

Frey left Odin's palace feeling sad and desolate. He knew that because Gerda was a Jotun, a daughter

Frey astride his golden boar, Gullinbursti *(Anthony Mercatante)*

of one of the hated GIANTS, and he, Frey, was Lord of the Elves, he could never win her. Besides, it was said that her heart was as frozen as a seed in the hard winter earth.

Frey was so unhappy that he could not eat, sleep, or speak. Everyone was troubled for him. Trees lost their leaves, and flowers faded. All nature mourned for Frey. At last Frey's father, Niord, sent Skirnir to speak to his son.

Skirnir was Frey's friend and trusted servant. It did not take him long to find out what troubled Frey. Skirnir said that he would go to woo the maiden for Frey if Frey would lend him BLODIGHOFI, the wondrous horse that could leap through fire unharmed, and Frey's magic sword that struck giants and trolls of its own accord.

Frey agreed, and Skirnir set off to JOTUNHEIM, the land of the giants. When he came to a wall of fire, Blodighofi leaped with Skirnir through the flames. They both came out unscathed.

Outside Gymir's hall huge hounds set up a fearsome barking, howling like the winds of winter. Skirnir asked an old shepherd for advice but the man offered no help. Instead he told Skirnir that he had no hope of winning Gerda, for her heart was made of ice. He said that Frey was doomed to failure and death.

Skirnir knew that the NORNS had decided his fate and when he should die. There was nothing he could do except to go about his duty with hope and courage.

Inside her hall, Gerda looked coldly at Skirnir. First he offered her golden apples if she would give her love to Frey, but Gerda had plenty of gold. Then he offered her Odin's magic ring, DRAUPNIR, but Gerda had plenty of jewels.

Next Skirnir tried threats: He would cut off her head with the magic sword. Gerda replied that her father would kill Skirnir first and keep the magic sword for himself. Skirnir followed by drawing from his belt a wand and a knife. He said he would carve the most terrifying magic RUNES upon the wand and strike her with it. The runes would be curses that doomed her to be forever lonely and filled with longing. She would have no friends, no husband, no children. Only the horrible frost giant HRIMGRIMNIR would pursue her with foul corpses for companions. Food and drink would taste loathsome to her. She would always be cold and miserable and would slowly dry up like a dying thistle, trampled underfoot and forgotten by all.

At this dreadful threat Gerda at last promised to marry Frey. Skirnir left Frey's magic sword behind as a bride price for Gymir and rode back to Frey with the happy news that Gerda would wed him in nine days at the sacred BARLEY patch, BARRI. (In Norse mythology nine days symbolize the nine months of a northern winter.) The long delay dismayed Frey until he should meet his bride.

It is said that after they were married Frey and Gerda were the happiest couple in the world, for the warmth of Frey's love had melted Gerda's icy heart, just as the sun of spring thaws the frozen earth and brings forth the plants from seeds hidden inside it.

The story of Frey and Gerda is a moving love poem. It exemplifies the deep longing the Norse had for the sunshine and warmth of spring after the long, frozen winters of their native lands.

**FREYA** (Lady)   The goddess of love and fertility. Freya was the daughter of the VANIR god NIORD and his sister-wife, NERTHUS, and the sister of FREY. Freya came to ASGARD with her brother and father after the WAR BETWEEN THE AESIR AND THE VANIR ended

Freya had a chariot pulled by two cats. *(Anthony Mercatante)*

in an eternal peace treaty. Freya's home in Asgard was in FOLKVANGER in a hall named SESSRUMNIR.

Freya was married to OD, but this mysterious character (whose name means "roamer") disappeared. Freya was said to roam the earth looking for him and shedding tears that turned to pure gold. Freya and Od had a daughter named HNOSSA, which means "jewel." Freya was exceedingly beautiful and many fell in love with her, including GIANTS, DWARFS, and HUMANS.

Like most of the Vanir, Freya had a talent for witchcraft. It is said that when she came to Asgard, she instructed the gods in the magical arts of SEID.

Freya also had a warlike side and shared Odin's love of battle. It is said that she and Odin divided the slain heroes between them so that some went to Odin's VALHALLA while others went to Sessrumnir. Freya's boar, the gold-bristled HILDISVINI, was a symbol of war. Its name means "Battle Boar."

Freya possessed a boar chariot and a chariot pulled by two gray or black CATS. She also had a FALCON skin that she sometimes donned to fly away. She lent the falcon skin to LOKI, the trickster god, in the stories "Idunn's Apples" (see under IDUNN) and "The Theft of Thor's Hammer" (see under THOR). Her most precious possession was the BRISINGAMEN.

The sixth day of the week, FRIDAY, is named after Freya.

**Freya, Ottar, and the Giantess Hyndla**  Freya, goddess of love and fertility, was loved by many, including the human male OTTAR. In the *LAY OF HYNDLA* (see *HYNDLULJOTH*) from the *POETIC EDDA*, Freya transforms Ottar into the shape of her boar, Hildisvini, and visits the giantess HYNDLA in her cave. Hyndla is a powerful seeress. Freya cajoles and bullies Hindla into telling Ottar all about his ancestors from far back so that he may win a wager with another mortal, Angantyr. In Norse times, it was very important to know one's lineage; proof of it was often used to settle disputes over land and other property. One of Ottar's ancestors turned out to be SIGURD, the greatest of Germanic heroes, so he was sure to win his bet.

Once Hyndla had finished reciting the list of Ottar's ancestors, she wanted to leave Freya and her "boar." Freya used witchcraft to persuade Hyndla to brew some "memory beer" for Ottar, so that he would remember every detail of what Hyndla had told him. Freya caused flames to dance around the giantess until she gave Ottar the brew.

**Freya and the Golden Necklace**  Freya had an enormous greed for gold and jewelry of all kinds. One day she went to the cave of the black DWARFS ALFRIGG, BERLING, DVALIN, and GRERR. These master craftsmen had made a golden necklace of outstanding beauty. Freya knew at once that she would do anything to get the necklace that the dwarfs called the Brisingamen.

She offered the dwarfs gold and silver, but as Dvalin pointed out, they already had all the precious metals and gems of the underworld for the taking. Freya began to weep golden tears. At last Dvalin said they would give her the necklace if she would agree to spend a day and a night with each of the dwarfs. Freya was so overcome with greed that she gave herself to the company of the four ugly little creatures for four days and four nights. When she went back to her palace at Folkvanger, she was wearing the Brisingamen around her neck.

Now Loki, the mischief maker, had followed Freya to SVARTALFHEIM, the home of the dwarfs, and had seen everything that had happened. He ran to tell ODIN. Odin was furious when he heard the story. He bade Loki to take the necklace from Freya and bring it to him.

Loki had a hard time getting into Freya's sleeping chamber at Sessrumnir, her palace, for all the doors and windows were tightly shut. At last the shape-changer turned himself into a small fly and entered the room through a hole as small as a needle's eye. Loki saw that Freya was wearing the necklace around her neck, with the clasp underneath her so that he could not reach it. Never at a loss, Loki turned himself into a flea and bit the goddess on her cheek. She turned restlessly in her sleep and exposed the clasp. Quickly Loki turned back into his own shape, removed the necklace, unlocked the door, and crept out.

When Freya discovered her loss she ran to Odin and told her story, weeping bitterly. Cold with anger at Freya's tale of greed and lust, Odin said that he would retrieve the jewel for her only if she would agree to stir

Freya visited the dwarfs to obtain the Brisingamen, her golden necklace. (*Anthony Mercatante*)

up a terrible war between two powerful chieftains on Earth. He demanded that there should be killing and bloodshed. Afterward Freya should bring the slain heroes back to life. Freya willingly agreed to the terms, for like Odin, she had the gift of sorcery and a lust for battle and heroes. Then Odin sent for HEIMDALL, the watchman of the gods, and told him to go after Loki and bring back Freya's trinket.

Loki turned himself into a seal and swam to a rock near SINGASTEIN, but a moment later Heimdall, too, had become a seal. The two fought a fierce battle. In the end Heimdall, with the necklace in his hand, led the dripping Loki out of the water and back to Odin.

The story of the Brisingamen is from the 10th-century skaldic poem *Husdrapa* and the 15th-century *Flateyjarbok* (Book of the Flat Island).

**FRIDAY**  In English, Friday, the sixth day of the week, takes its name from FREYA, the Norse goddess of love and fertility.

**FRIGG** (FRIGGA, FRIJA)  The chief AESIR goddess; wife of ODIN; daughter of FJORGYN (1), the earth goddess. Frigg herself is called EARTH MOTHER. She is associated with love, marriage, and motherhood. Frigg is frequently pictured as being very beautiful, wearing a girdle hung with household keys and weaving clouds on her spinning wheel. Eleven handmaidens attended her in her hall, FENSALIR. Frigg was the mother of BALDER, and according to some sources, she was also the mother of THOR, the thunder god, and of HODUR, the blind god who unwittingly slew Balder.

Because of the fragmentary nature of the Norse EDDAS and SAGAS, there are conflicting views of Frigg. Besides her portrayal as a devoted wife and mother, Frigg also appears as a sorceress who wears a falcon skin and sees into the future, and as a wanton woman who covets gold and jewelry and the love of men. She and the goddess FREYA have a lot in common. Some believe that they are various facets of the same deity.

Frigg, attended by her handmaidens, spun clouds on her spindle. *(Anthony Mercatante)*

**FULLA** (FYLLR, FYLLA; Bountiful)  One of the female goddesses, or ASYNJUR, named by 13th century Icelandic writer SNORRI STURLUSON in his work GYLFAGINNING. Fulla wore her hair loose, with a golden band around her head. A virgin, Fulla served the goddess FRIGG by carrying her basket, tending her shoes, and keeping her secrets. Fulla was one of the three goddesses to whom the dead god BALDER sent gifts from HEL. She received a gold ring.

Some scholars believe Fulla was an ancient goddess of fertility modified over time into the smaller role of Frigg's servant.

**FYLGIE** (Follower)  As well as the NORNS, or Fates, the Norse ascribed to each human being a guardian spirit or double, which accompanied a person throughout his or her life. The Fylgie had a human or animal shape but was invisible except in dreams or at the moment of death. When the Fylgie appeared to a person who was awake, it was a sign of that person's death. When a person died, the Fylgie passed on to another member of the family.

# G

**GAGNRAD** One of the many names used by the god ODIN. He used this one when he went to visit the wise giant Vafthrudnir (see *VAFTHRUDNISMAL.*)

**GALAR** One of the two DWARFS (the other was FJALAR [2]) who killed the wise man KVASIR and collected his blood to make the MEAD of poetry (see under ODIN).

**GANG** One of the storm giants, brother of THIAZZI and IDI. Their father, OLVALDI, had left piles of gold to be divided among his sons (see "Skade and Niord," under SKADE).

**GANGLATI** HEL's slow-moving manservant in ELJUDNIR, Hel's hall in the underworld.

**GANGLOT** HEL's slow-moving woman servant in ELJUDNIR, Hel's hall in the underworld.

**GARM** The fearsome, howling hound who stood at the gates of HEL's realm, guarding the kingdom of the dead. In some stories, Garm could be quieted only by a piece of cake given to him by those who had already given bread to the poor. In *The Lay of Grimnir* (see GRIMNISMAL), Garm is described as the fiercest of all hounds. In "Balder's Dreams" (see under BALDER), when ODIN went to the underworld to consult a seeress, the blood-caked hound of Hel howled at him, but Odin went on, undeterred by the hideous noise. At RAGNAROK Garm fought with one-handed TYR, and they killed each other. Garm is sometimes thought to be another name for the WOLF FENRIR.

**GEFION** (Giver) A goddess of fertility, associated with the plow. In one myth told by SNORRI STURLUSON in the *PROSE EDDA*, Gefion disguised herself as a beggarwoman. She asked GYLFI, the king of SWEDEN, to give her some land. The king told her that she could have as much land as she could plow in a day and a night. The old woman went off to find her four sons, who were huge oxen that had been fathered by a giant. Gefion hitched the oxen to a plow and proceeded to cut deeply into the land of Sweden. Then she and the oxen towed the land into the sea where it is now known as the island of Zealand, part of DENMARK.

**GEIRROD (1)** The giant who, with the help of the trickster god LOKI, persuaded the god THOR to visit him without his famous weapons. It was a trap, but thanks to the friendly giantess GRID, Thor was able to kill Geirrod and his two ogress daughters, GIALF and GREIP.

**GEIRROD (2)** Son of King HRAUDING and brother of AGNAR. Geirrod betrayed his brother and took his throne. Later he killed himself by falling upon his own sword, as ODIN, his benefactor, had prophesied in *GRIMNISMAL* ("Lay of Grimnir").

**Geirrod and Agnar** The two brothers, Geirrod and Agnar were the sons of King Hrauding of the Goths. When the children were eight and 10 years old, respectively, their little fishing boat was wrecked in a storm. The boys landed on an island and were taken care of by an old couple who were Odin and FRIGG in disguise. Frigg took special care of Agnar and Odin took care of Geirrod, giving them many words of advise before sending them back to their own land. As their boat approached shore, Geirrod leaped out, taking the oars with him, and shoved the boat back out to sea. Geirrod was welcomed home, and because his father had died, he became king in place of Agnar, who was presumed dead.

Many years went by before Odin and Frigg thought about the two boys they had rescued from the sea. Then Odin boasted that his foster son, Geirrod, was king of a great country, while Frigg's Agnar was a nobody who lived in a cave. Frigg retorted that Geirrod was mean and treacherous. When Odin decided to go to MIDGARD to test Geirrod, Frigg sent her maidservant, FULLA, to warn Geirrod that he was not to trust the visitor who was coming to him, wearing a sky-blue cape.

Geirrod heeded the warning. Odin arrived wearing a sky-blue cape. He called himself GRIMNIR, but more than that he would not say. In a fit of rage at what he considered insolence, Geirrod had Grimnir slung between two fires. There he stayed for eight days and nights, without food or drink. Then Agnar, the son of Geirrod, named after his lost uncle, took pity on Odin-Grimnir and quenched his thirst with ale.

Grimnir began to chant a song that was known as *Grimnismal (The Lay of Grimnir)*. The song contained a great deal of knowledge about ASGARD, the home of the gods, and about the gods themselves and their possessions, especially about Odin and his many names. When Geirrod finally realized that his captive was Odin, he leapt up to release him, but he fell on his own sword and killed himself. Then Odin disappeared, and Geirrod's son, Agnar, became king and ruled for many peaceable years.

**GELGJA** The name that 13th-century Icelandic writer SNORRI STURLUSON gave to a very strong chain used to help secure FENRIR, the giant, monstrous WOLF. After learning that Fenrir, a son of the god LOKI, would eventually help destroy them, the gods decided to chain the wolf to a huge rock and keep him captive forever. Finally, through magic, they managed to get the rope GLEIPNIR around the wolf's neck. They fastened Gleipnir to Gelgja, a shackle or chain. Some experts believe Gelgja, too, was made of magical materials. Finally, the gods fastened Gelgja to the rock GIOLL (1).

**GERDA** (GERD; Enclosed Field) The daughter of the JOTUN GYMIR and AURBODA, the sister of BELI, and the wife of FREY, whose servant SKIRNIR, wooed and won the giantess for his master. Gerda spurned apples and gold but finally gave in at the terrible threat of eternal cold and loneliness, thus personifying winter giving in at last to the warm sunshine of spring. The nine nights of waiting between her consent to become Frey's bride and the actual union is symbolic of the long nine months of hard winter, in northern countries, before spring arrives. In some mythologies the radiance of Gerda personifies the AURORA BOREALIS (northern lights).

**GERI** (Ravenous) One of the WOLF companions of the god ODIN. The other was FREKI, whose name also means "ravenous." Odin fed the wolves all the meat that was served to him, for he needed only to drink divine MEAD for sustenance. The wolves attended him at HLIDSKIALF, his high seat, and also at VALHALLA.

**GESTA DANORUM** A 16-volume history of the Danish people from prehistoric days to the 13th century written by SAXO GRAMMATICUS, a Danish scholar and historian. Books 10 through 16 are strictly historical, and scholars believe Saxo wrote these first. Books 1 through 9 record the oral myths and legends of the NORSE people, who included those living in DENMARK. Saxo apparently learned these stories from well-educated and well-traveled men from ICELAND. The *Gesta Danorum* is considered a very important source of information on the legends, myths, and religions of the Scandinavians.

**GIALAR** (GJALLAR; Ringing Horn) The trumpet horn of the god HEIMDALL that sounded throughout the NINE WORLDS. Heimdall sometimes left Gialar beside MIMIR'S WELL. At RAGNAROK, the end of the world, the sound of Gialar would summon gods and men to battle.

Gialar is usually pictured as a *lur*, the ancient bronze trumpet of SCANDINAVIA, dating back to about 1000 B.C. *Lurs* were made in pairs, twisting in opposite directions so that the two held side by side looked like the horns of a large animal. Some *lurs* have been excavated from the peat bogs of DENMARK and can still be played.

**GIALLARBRU** (GJALLARBRU) The bridge that crosses the river GIOLL (2) and connects the worlds of the living with the worlds of the dead. The god HERMOD must cross the Giallarbru to rescue the spirit of the recently deceased BALDER, son of ODIN and FRIGG.

## GIALP (GJALP; Howler)

Daughter of the giant GEIRROD (1), and sister of GREIP. She tried to drown the god THOR and, later, to crush him to death against the roof rafters, but Thor killed Gialp and her sister.

## GIANT MASTER BUILDER

The giant who tricked the gods into hiring him to build a new wall around ASGARD, intended to protect the gods from the GIANTS. The old wall had been destroyed in the war with the VANIR. This unnamed giant took the form of an ordinary builder and traveled to Asgard, his great stallion pulling a wagon. He told the gods he could complete the job for them in three years if they paid him by giving him the SUN AND MOON and the fertility goddess, FREYA. Mischief maker LOKI persuaded the gods to accept the offer under the condition that the builder complete the task in less than half a year. The giant accepted the new terms. Once the builder started working, the gods discovered that he was a giant, aided by a giant stallion. They grew dismayed and fearful that they might indeed lose their goddess and the Sun and Moon in a very bad arrangement. Three days before the wall was completed, Loki, the SHAPE-SHIFTER, turned himself into a mare and lured the stallion away from the construction site, thereby spoiling the giant's plan.

## GIANTS

Giants play a central role in Norse mythology, mainly as the enemy of the gods but also as the race from which the gods most likely were offspring. The different roles that giants play in the surviving stories are so confusing that some experts suggest that in Norse religious beliefs, the giants were gods themselves or perhaps the gods were giants.

The giant YMIR was the first being in the cosmos, according to 13th-century writer SNORRI STURLUSON's version of the Norse CREATION myth. Details from Snorri's PROSE EDDA tell how Ymir evolved from the heat and cold in the beginning times, and from the parts of his body were born the JOTUN (giants) and the HRIMTHURSSAR (frost giants). At the same time that Ymir came into being, the first cow, AUD-

HUMLA, formed out of the chaos. She licked at a salt block and uncovered BURI, whose son BOR mated with BESTLA, one of the first giantesses. From these latter two, one a giant, came the first gods: ODIN, VILI, and VE.

This shared ancestry of gods and giants has caused much curiosity among modern scholars, though no answers to the puzzle exist in surviving records. Most commonly, the giants are interpreted as representing the wild forces of nature that threatened people living in northern climates more so than those in southern lands. The giants lived in mountains and often hurled huge boulders at one another. They loved darkness and often confronted the gods at night. (See also JOTUN.)

## GILLING

The giant killed by the dwarfs FJALAR and GALAR (see "The Mead of Poetry," under ODIN). He was the father of SUTTUNG.

## GIMLÉ

The court of the gods after the end of the world (see "Regeneration," under RAGNAROK). Stories describe Gimlé as fairer than the Sun and roofed in gold. There the rulers would live at peace with one another.

## GINNUNGAGAP

The gaping pit that lay between NIFLHEIM (the place of mists and ice) and MUSPELLHEIM (the world of raging fire). It existed before land or sea, heaven or Earth. It was in Ginnungagap that the first living creatures were formed: YMIR, the first giant, and AUDHUMLA, the cow (see CREATION).

## GIOLL (1) (GJOLL)

The rock to which the bonds of the WOLF FENRIR were attached after the gods had captured him.

## GIOLL (2) (GJOLL)

The river that divides the worlds of the living from the afterlife. The bridge GIALLARBRU crosses this river. The god HERMOD crossed the Gioll over Giallarbru as he hurried to rescue the spirit of BALDER, ODIN's son, shortly after Balder's death.

## GIOTUNAGARD (GRJOTUNAGARDAR, GRIOTUNAGARD; Place of Stones, Stone Fence

House) The place where the duel between the god THOR and the giant HRUNGNIR took place.

**GLADSHEIM** (Joyous Home) The hall in ASGARD where all the AESIR gods had their high seats or thrones. It was thatched in silver and stood in the green plain of IDAVOLL. The principal seat, HLID-SKIALF, was that of the god ODIN.

**GLEIPNIR** The magic chain made by the DWARFS to bind FENRIR, the WOLF.

**GLITNIR** The hall of FORSETI, who was the son of the god BALDER. Forseti dwelled in this hall of gold and silver and helped settle arguments and fights.

**GNA** One of the minor goddesses of the AESIR, according to 13th-century writer SNORRI STURLUSON. Gna ran errands for the goddess FRIGG, ODIN's wife. When she needed to deliver a message in a hurry, Gna rode her horse, Hofvarpnir (Hoof-Thrasher), through the air. Her Old NORSE name came to refer to very high things or something that soars high.

**GOAT** A mammal related to the sheep family. In Norse mythology the god THOR had a cart drawn by two billy goats, TANNGNIOST and TANNGRISNIR. These goats could be killed and eaten and then revived again the next day.

**GOTHS** A Germanic tribe that in the third and fifth centuries invaded and settled in parts of the Roman Empire.

In the story "Geirrod and Agnar" (see under GEIRROD [2]), HRAUDING was king of the Goths. His son Geirrod succeeded him.

**GOTLAND** An island in the Baltic Sea, part of SWEDEN and southeast of that nation's coast. Many archaeological finds that are important to the study of Norse mythology are located on this large island. Most prominent are the rock carvings and pictures that appear to portray scenes from Norse myths. They are similar to the rock carvings found throughout much of SCANDINAVIA.

In one set of rocks on Gotland, the background was carved away leaving the images raised above the surface. Archaeologists believe the images were carved in the sixth century A.D. and were originally painted. One famous raised picture stone from Alskog Tjangvide shows what appears to be SLEIPNIR, ODIN's eight-legged horse. The carving has been dated the eighth century A.D.

**GREIP** (Grasper) Daughter of the giant GEIR-ROD (1) and sister of GIALP. The giant sisters tried to kill the god THOR but were instead crushed to death by him.

**GRERR** One of the four dwarfs who made the BRISINGAMEN for the goddess FREYA. The others were ALFRIGG, BERLING, and DVALIN.

**GRID** The giantess who was one of the wives of the god ODIN and the mother of their son, VIDAR. Friendly to the gods, she helped THOR by lending him her magic gloves, girdle, and staff when Thor visited the giant GEIRROD (1). Some legends say that she also made the shoe that Vidar wore at RAGNAROK to slay the wolf FENRIR.

**GRIM** (GRIMNR) One of the god ODIN's many nicknames. It is found in many English place-names (for example Grim's Ditch, Grim's Dyke, Grimsby, and Grimesthorpe).

**GRIMNIR** (Hooded One) One of the god ODIN's many names. When he went to MIDGARD to visit his foster son, GEIRROD (2), Odin wore a sky-blue hooded cape. Odin chanted the GRIMNISMAL, while he was held captive at the hall of Geirrod.

**GRIMNISMAL** (*The Lay of Grimnir*) GRIMNIR, who was the god ODIN in disguise, was captured by GEIRROD (2) and tied between two fires. Geirrod's son, Agnar, quenched Grimnir's thirst with horns of ale, and Odin rewarded him by singing this lay.

Grimnir's song told of the halls of the gods in their realm, ASGARD, including YDALIR, GLADSHEIM, and especially VALHALLA, with details about the hall itself and the cook, boar, and sooty cauldron in which the boar was cooked to feed the slain heroes of Valhalla. It also told of Odin's animal companions, the WOLF and the RAVEN, and of VALGRIND, Valhalla's outer gate, through which 800 warriors could march, side by side.

The song continues about Valhalla and then names all the rivers of the HVERGELMIR. The song explains how the gods gallop over BIFROST, the RAINBOW BRIDGE, to meet the council at the well URDARBRUNN. It also tells of the World Tree, YGGDRASIL, and of those who prey upon it. It mentions the names of the VALKYRIES who wait upon the dead heroes of Valhalla.

Other features of the song include the names of the horses that draw the chariots of the Sun and Moon, the terrible wolves that chased the chariots, the giant YMIR and how his flesh and bones and hair created Earth (see CREATION), and *TREASURES OF THE DWARFS*. And finally the captive Grimnir tells of the many names of Odin. It is then that Geirrod realizes that his prisoner is the great god Odin himself. Geirrod rises up to release his prisoner but falls upon his own sword and kills himself.

*Grimnismal* was a mnemonic poem (a sort of memory bank) for storytellers, poets, and minstrels who passed on information about myths, legends, and folktales to people from one generation to another, and in different communities all over SCANDINAVIA. Much of the information in *Grimnismal* is not found elsewhere. *Grimnismal* is part of the *POETIC EDDA* and is quoted by SNORRI STURLUSON.

**GROA**    The wife of AURVANDIL the Brave and mother of SVIPDAG, who visited her for advice in NIFLHEIM after her death in the poem *SVIPDAGSMAL*, part of the *POETIC EDDA*. In another story Groa uses her magic spells to cure THOR's headache but fails to remove the whetstone fragments from his skull.

**GULLFAXI** (Golden Mane)    The giant HRUNGNIR's powerful stallion that was defeated in a race by the god ODIN on his steed, eight-legged SLEIPNIR. Gullfaxi was then given to MAGNI, a son of the god THOR.

**GULLINBURSTI** (Golden Bristles)    The golden BOAR made by the DWARFS BROKK and EITI from a pigskin and thousands of pieces of gold wire, and given to the god FREY (see TREASURES OF THE DWARFS). Frey could ride on the boar or hitch his wagon to it, and Gullinbursti would speed across the Earth, sky, or sea faster than any horse. Its golden rays shone like the Sun and made plants grow everywhere. With its tusks Gullinbursti raked the earth and showed men how to plow the land.

Warriors wore the image of Frey's golden boar on helmets and shields as protection and good luck. Archaeologists found a seventh-century helmet topped by a boar in Benty Grange, in Derbyshire, England.

**GULLINKAMBI** (Golden Comb)    The bright red rooster that crowed to the gods and heroes at VALHALLA to tell them that RAGNAROK had begun.

**GULLINTANI** (Golden-Toothed)    A name sometimes given to HEIMDALL, who was supposed to have golden teeth and, hence, a dazzling smile.

**GULLTOPP** (Golden Tuft, Gold Top)    One of the 10 horses the AESIR gods rode each day to YGGDRASIL, the World Tree, which grew at the center of the universe. The gods came here on horseback each day to sit in judgment at the spring, or well, named URDARBRUNN. Gulltopp is the only horse to be named in the poems that tell of this journey. According to SNORRI STURLUSON, Gulltopp belongs to HEIMDALL, the god of light and guardian of the gods.

**GULLWEIG** (GULLVEIG; Power of Gold)    The beautiful witch who came to ASGARD and was probably the cause of the WAR BETWEEN THE AESIR AND THE VANIR. The AESIR burned her three times, but she rose up each time to cause trouble among the gods. Also called HEID (Shining One), Gullweig is thought by most scholars to be an aspect of the VANIR goddess FREYA, who also loved gold and had magical powers.

**GUNGNIR**    ODIN's magic spear, made by the DWARF sons of Ivaldi. Gungnir never missed its mark. It was a symbol of Odin as the god of war. Odin flung his spear at the VANIR gods in the WAR BETWEEN THE AESIR AND THE VANIR. Norse warriors threw their spears at the start of a battle to invoke Odin's protection in war.

**GUNLOD** (GUNNLOD)    Daughter of the giant SUTTUNG, who commanded Gunlod to guard the

MEAD of poetry, made from the blood of KVASIR. She became a wife of ODIN when he visited the cave on HNITBORG Mountain to steal the mead. She bore Odin a child, BRAGI, who went to ASGARD and became the god of poetry and the husband of IDUNN.

## GYLFAGINNING *(The Deceiving, or Beguiling, of Gylfi)* One of four main parts of the PROSE EDDA written by the 13th-century Icelandic historian, scholar, and chief SNORRI STURLUSON. Some scholars argue that *Gylfaginning* is Snorri's most important work.

The main character, GYLFI, a king of SWEDEN, disguises himself as an old wayfarer when he comes across a magnificent hall. In the hall sit three beings on high chairs. A servant invites Gylfi to stay and talk with the three beings. He sits and begins asking questions of the beings, who, Snorri tells the readers, are actually gods calling themselves High One, Just-As-High, and Third. Snorri uses the question-and-answer session to teach his readers about the beginnings of all existence, the gods and goddesses, and the end of time.

Snorri draws heavily on the works in the older POETIC EDDA, most notably the VOLUSPA (or *The Sibyl's Vision*, as Snorri calls it) and GRIMNISMAL *(Lay of Grimnir)*, to present this account of many Norse myths.

## GYLFI King of SWEDEN who was tricked by the goddess GEFION into giving her some of his land. In another myth Gylfi travels to ASGARD, the home of the gods, where he meets three beings called High One, Just-As-High, and Third. He questions them about Asgard, its creation, the doings of the gods and goddesses, and the end of the world. The three figures answer his questions at length. The poet SNORRI STURLUSON uses this story about Gylfi as a way to begin GYLFAGINNING, the first part of the PROSE EDDA.

## GYMIR A JOTUN, or GIANT, and the father of GERDA, who became the wife of the shining god, FREY.

**HARBARD** (Gray Beard)   One of the god ODIN's many names. In the *Harbardsljoth*, or *Lay of Harbard*, Harbard is a ferryman with one eye, a big hat, and a cape. He arrogantly refuses to take THOR, who does not recognize him as Odin, across the water on his ferry. The two fling insults and taunts at each other, and in the end Thor has to find another way across. The *Lay of Harbard* appears in the CODEX REGIUS and a part of it is in the *Arnamagnean Codex*. Both of these works are included in the POETIC EDDA.

**HATI**   One of the names given to the terrible WOLF that pursued the chariot of the Moon across the heavens and devoured it at RAGNAROK, the end of the world (see "Sun and Moon," under CREATION). This wolf is also known as MANAGARM. The 13th-century Icelandic historian SNORRI STURLUSAN wrote that Hati is the son of Hrodvitnisson. Both names mean "famous wolf," which has led some experts to suggest that Hati, or Managarm, is the offspring of FENRIR, the monster wolf, himself son of the god LOKI. The existing manuscripts of the Norse age are unclear on the exact name of the wolf that chases the Moon.

Hati is also the name of a giant who appears as a character in Icelandic poems.

See also SKOLL.

**HAUSTLONG**   A poem by Thiodor of Hvini, a ninth- or 10th-century Norwegian poet. It describes pictures painted on a shield thus is called a SKALDIC POEM, or shield poem.

The surviving 20 verses of *Haustlong* are preserved in the PROSE EDDA. Thirteen of the verses tell the myth of IDUNN and THIAZZI; seven describe THOR's duel with HRUNGNIR. Both stories portray gods carrying out bold exploits against the GIANTS of JOTUNHEIM.

**HAVAMAL** (*Words of the High One*)   A poem, part of the POETIC EDDA. Havamal contains many proverbs and advice on good living from the High One, who is the god ODIN. Some of it is addressed to the mortal LODDFAFNIR. *Havamal* also contains the lament of Odin for BILLING's daughter and the story of how Odin obtained the MEAD of poetry.

**HEID** (Shining One)   Another name for GULLWEIG, a witch or seeress. Gullweig called herself Heid when she used her magic or powers to see into the future.

**HEIDRUN** (HEITHRON)   The lively shegoat who nibbled the leaves of LAERAD, the tree of VALHALLA. She produced a never-ending supply of MEAD for the gods and heroes at their nightly feasts in ODIN's hall.

**HEIMDALL**   WATCHMAN OF THE GODS. Heimdall was mysteriously born of nine mothers and the god ODIN. Heimdall was tall and handsome, with a dazzling smile. He was sometimes called the god of light, the shining god, or the white god.

Heimdall had a wonderful horn called GIALAR, whose blast could be heard all over the NINE WORLDS, and that Heimdall blew at RAGNAROK, the end of the world. His horse was GULLTOP (Golden Tuft), and his sword was HOFUND. He lived in a fortresslike hall called HIMINBJORG (Cliffs of Heaven).

Heimdall had amazing abilities. His eyesight was so sharp that he could see for 100 miles all around him. Some said he could see even farther or that he had "second sight" that allowed him to see into the future. It is certain that he saw all the comings and goings of those who crossed BIFROST, the RAINBOW

Heimdall, the watchman of the gods, rides Gulltop and brandishes his horn, Gialar. *(Historical Picture Service–Chicago)*

BRIDGE that led from ASGARD, the home of the gods, to MIDGARD (Middle Earth).

Heimdall spotted sly LOKI from afar, after the trickster god had stolen FREYA's necklace and escaped with it into the sea, where he changed himself into a sleek seal. Heimdall, too, was able to change his shape. He dived, seal-like, into the water, barking and nipping. Heimdall vanquished Loki and took the necklace back to Freya. He and Loki were enemies from then on and in the end would kill each other at RAGNAROK.

Heimdall was clever, too. He had the brilliant idea of sending the thunder god, THOR, to JOTUNHEIM dressed as a girl in bridal dress in order to get back Thor's magic hammer from the giant THRYM, who had stolen it.

Heimdall's hearing was so acute and finely tuned that he could hear the grass pushing up from under the earth and the wool growing on a sheep's back. Heimdall needed so little sleep that it seemed he was always awake and alert.

**Heimdall's Nine Mothers**  One obscure and fragmented myth, related in the HYNDLULJOTH of the POETIC EDDA, told the following story about the origins of Heimdall, the watchman of the bridge Bifrost.

One day when the great god Odin walked along the seashore, he came across nine beautiful giantesses, sound asleep on the sand. They were the wave maidens, daughters of the sea god, AEGIR. Their names were Alta (Fury), Augeia (Sand Strewer), Aurgiafa (Sorrow-Whelmer), Egia (Foamer), GIALP (Howler), GREIP (Gripper), JARNSAXA (Ironstone), Sindur (Dusk), and Ulfrum (She-Wolf). Odin was so enchanted with their beauty that he wedded all nine of them, and together the nine giantesses brought forth a beautiful son named Heimdall.

The nine mothers nurtured their son on the strength of the earth, the moisture of the sea, and the heat of the Sun. The new god thrived so well on this diet that he was soon tall enough and strong enough to hasten to ASGARD, the home of the gods.

There, the gods endowed Heimdall with marvelously keen senses and a trumpet called Gialar, and named him guardian of the Rainbow Bridge, Bifrost.

**HEL** (HELA; Hell)   The goddess of death and the underworld. Hel was the daughter of the god LOKI and the ogress ANGRBODA. Her brothers were FENRIR, the wolf, and JORMUNGAND, the Midgard Serpent.

According to SNORRI STURLUSON, Hel was terrible to look at, for one-half of her was greenish black and the other a livid white, with flesh that seemed to be rotting like that of a corpse, and her face was gloomy, grim, and sinister.

The great god ODIN cast Hel down to NIFLHEIM, the realm of cold darkness and death. He bade her

Hel, queen of the underworld, is shown here with her hound, Garm. *(Illustration by Johannes Gehrts, Anthony Mercatante Collection)*

look after all the wicked and miserable souls who had died of sickness, corruption, and old age. (Dead heroes went to Odin's glorious hall, VALHALLA.) Hel's palace was called ELJUDNIR, and here she entertained the dead in a grisly kind of way: Her table was called Hunger; her knife, Starvation; her bed, Sickness; and the curtains around it, Misfortune.

It was said that in times of famine and plague Hel left her ghastly realm to roam the Earth on her three-legged white horse and to rake up the survivors and sweep them with her broom down to Niflheim.

Although the gods looked upon her with loathing, Hel had more power than Odin; once someone was in her power, no one, not even Odin, could reclaim that soul unless Hel gave her permission. In the story of BALDER, who was killed and went to Niflheim, Hel refused to give him up, even though Odin and FRIGG sent the god HERMOD to plead and bargain with her.

The early Christians so feared Hel that they borrowed her name to describe the place of everlasting torment reserved for the souls of the wicked—Hell.

**HERMOD**   Son of ODIN and FRIGG. Hermod was bold and brave. It was he who volunteered to go to HEL's underworld and beg her to release his dead brother, BALDER. In some versions of the myths, Hermod also goes at Odin's bidding to visit the wizard ROSTIOFF in Lapland (see "Vali, the Avenger," under VALI). Hermod stands at Odin's side at the gates of VALHALLA to welcome the dead heroes.

**HILDISVINI** (Battle Boar)   The goddess FREYA's BOAR. His golden bristles showed the way in the dark. He was created for Freya by the dwarfs DAIN (1) and NABBI. Freya's human lover, OTTAR, took the form of Hildisvini to visit, with Freya, the giantess HYNDLA.

**HIMINBJORG** (Cliffs of Heaven, Heaven Mountain)   The eighth great hall, or palace, in ASGARD, kingdom of the AESIR god. Himinbjorg is the home of the god HEIMDALL. The palace stands near BIFROST, the bridge between heaven and Earth. From his vantage point overlooking this passage between the three worlds of the universe, Heimdall carries out his duty to watch over the lives of the other gods.

Hermod, atop Odin's eight-legged steed, Sleipnir, rides to the underworld to try to rescue Balder from the dead. *(New York Public Library Picture Collection)*

**HIMINBRIOTER** (Heaven Bellower, Sky Bellower) The black ox killed by THOR and used as bait to catch JORMUNGAND, the Midgard Serpent.

**"HJADNINGAVIG"** ("Battle of the Followers of Hedin") A story of endless battle preserved in three separate sources: a SKALDIC POEM written in the ninth century by Bragi Boddason, the 13th-century works of Icelandic writer SNORRI STURLUSON, and most fully in the late 14th-century SAGA *Sorlathattra*.

Through the magic of the goddess FREYA or an unknown witch, the armies of two kings, Hogni and Hedin Hjarrandason, engage in a battle that goes on day after day for 143 years. The war begins after Hedin abducts Hild, Hogni's beautiful daughter. Hedin is about to return the woman but is too late, for Hogni has already drawn the dread sword, DAINSLEIF, which must kill a man before it can be returned to its sheath. Each day the warriors fight. At night, the magic restores even the most severely injured, those who would normally die in a battle that was not bewitched.

According to some sources the end of this tedious battle comes at RAGNAROK, the final war between the GIANTS and the gods at the end of time. Others say it ends with the arrival of King Olaf I Tryggvason, who ruled NORWAY from A.D. 995 to 1001 and forced the conversion of many people to Christianity. Modern scholars see parallels or opposites between the horror described in this battle and glorious life of the EINHERJAR, the souls of HUMAN warriors in VALHALLA.

**HLESEY** The island under which the sea giant, AEGIR, and his wife, RAN, lived in their coral cave. Experts believe actual site of Hlesey may be the island of Laeso, in the Kattegat (cat's throat), a strait between the islands of Jutland and Zealand in DENMARK.

**HLIDSKIALF** (LIDSKJALF; High Seat) ODIN's throne in the high tower of his palace, VALASKIALF, in ASGARD, the home of the gods. From here Odin could see all that occurred in the NINE WORLDS. He had his RAVENS, HUGIN and MUNIN, to help him, and the wolves GERI and FREKI to keep him company. No one but Odin was allowed to sit on Hlidskialf with the exception of his wife FRIGG. The god FREY,

though, once disobeyed the rules. From the high perch he spotted the JOTUN maid GERDA and fell in love with her.

**HLIN** (Protectress) One of the minor goddesses of the AESIR, according to 13th-century Icelandic historian SNORRI STURLUSON. FRIGG assigned Hlin the job of protecting from danger anyone Frigg chose. The name Hlin appears often in the poem VOLUSPA, but her character remains unclear to modern scholars.

**HNITBORG** The mountain stronghold where the giant SUTTUNG hid the MEAD of poetry (see under ODIN), which he had stolen. Suttung's daughter, GUNLOD, stood guard over the vessels containing the mead.

**HNOSSA** (NOSSA) The daughter of the goddess FREYA and OD. Her name means "jewel." SNORRI STURLUSON wrote that she was so beautiful that her name could be given to anything that is precious or lovely.

**HODDMIMIR'S WOOD** Another name for the sacred tree YGGDRASIL, used in *VAFTHRUDNISMAL* (*Lay of Vafthrudnir*). It was from Hoddmimir's Wood that the two humans LIF and LIFTHRASIR emerged at the end of the world, after RAGNAROK.

**HODUR** (HOD) The blind god. His father was ODIN; his mother, FRIGG; and his brother, BALDER. Hodur unwittingly killed Balder with the help of the trickster god LOKI, and a sprig of MISTLETOE. Hodur in turn was killed by VALI, the avenger, another son of Odin. After RAGNAROK (the end of the world), Hodur and Balder were reconciled and together returned from HEL's underworld to the new world.

**HOENIR** (HONIR) The god of silence. He was one of the three original AESIR gods who, along with his brothers ODIN and LOTHUR created the world (see CREATION). In his *PROSE EDDA*, SNORRI STURLUSON calls him VILI and Lothur VE.

After the WAR BETWEEN THE AESIR AND THE VANIR, Hoenir went to live with the VANIR as part of an exchange of gods. With him went the wise MIMIR. The Vanir gods became angry when Hoenir appeared to be indecisive and not quick-witted, always relying on Mimir to make decisions. Because Hoenir was Odin's brother the Vanir did not harm him but instead killed Mimir and sent his head back to Odin.

Hoenir is associated with Odin and LOKI in the stories "Idunn's Apples" (see under IDUNN) and "Otr's Ransom" (see under OTR), when he accompanied the two gods on journeys to Earth.

Hoenir survived RAGNAROK, the end of the world. Not much is known about this silent god.

## HOFUND  The sword of the god HEIMDALL.

## HORSE  The horse plays an important role as helper in Norse mythology, but archaeological and historical evidence suggests that the ancient people of SCANDINAVIA also worshiped the horse. The Germanic tribes that were the ancestors to the NORSE regarded horses as mouthpieces of the gods and tried to learn about the future from their snorts and neighs. Evidence from Scandinavia suggests that the Norse sacrificed large numbers of horses and even made horses fight each other as a way of determining which to sacrifice. People also saw a link between horses and fertility.

Horses provided a medium for the gods to travel between the lands of the living and the dead. Famous horses in Norse mythology include ODIN's eight-legged horse, SLEIPNIR, and GULLTOPP, the horse HEIMDALL rode to warn the gods of the coming of RAGNAROK.

## HRAFNAGALDUR ODINS (Odin's Raven Chant)
An Old NORSE poem that was once considered part of the *POETIC EDDA* but has long been left out of editions and translations of those poems. *Hrafnagaldur Odins* is preserved in several 17th-century manuscripts now in the royal libraries in Stockholm, NORWAY, and Copenhagen, DENMARK. Since the late 1800s when an expert declared it to be a forgery, *Hrafnagaldur Odins* has received little scholarly attention. Research by Old Norse experts working in the late 20th and early 21st centuries, however, has contradicted that much older opinion. Some modern experts now include this poem as part of the *Poetic Edda*.

*Hrafnagaldur Odins* is proving to be a confusing poem for scholars to interpret and understand.

Essentially, it tells the story of the gods' visit to the underworld and their questioning of a goddess who dwells there.

## HRAUDING  King of the Goths, father of GEIR-ROD (2) and AGNAR.

## HREIDMAR (REIDMAR)  A master magician. His sons were REGIN, FAFNIR, and OTR. His daughters were LOFNHEID and LYNGHEID. Otr was killed by the trickster god, LOKI. As compensation for his son's death, Hreidmar was given the DWARF ANDVARI's treasure of gold. Hreidmar was killed by Fafnir, who stole the treasure and turned himself into a dragon.

## HRIMFAXI (Frosty Mane)  The name of NOTT's horse, from whose bit fell the froth that nightly bedewed the Earth (see "Night and Day," under CREATION).

## HRIMGRIMNIR (RIMEGRIM; Frost Mask)  The frost giant who will pursue GERDA if she refuses to marry FREY. He is the personification of the cruel cold of northern winters.

## HRIMTHURSSAR  The frost GIANTS who lived in JOTUNHEIM, enemies of the gods. The Hrimthurssar represented the changing seasons and the coming of the eternal night, cold, and danger of the long winters of northern climates. Their names represent the harshness of winter: THIAZZI (Ice), THRYM (Frost), SKADE (Destruction), Jokull (Glacier), Frosti (Cold), and others.

The Hrimthurssar are descendants of YMIR, the first great giant, formed from the ice and fire that existed at the beginning of time. Ymir represented, in part, the numbing cold of the Artic.

## HRINGHORNI (Ring Horn)  The longship of the god BALDER. It was perhaps named for the intricate curving ring designs with which it (like many Norse ships) was adorned. When Balder was slain, the funeral pyre for his body was built on *Hringhorni*. THOR set the fire ablaze, and the ship was sent out to sea.

See also SHIPS AND SHIP BURIALS.

**HRUNGNIR** Strongest of the GIANTS; described as large and stone-headed. Hrungnir bet his horse GULLFAXI (Golden Mane) in a race with ODIN's eight-legged steed SLEIPNIR. He lost the race, then engaged in a duel with THOR, in which he was killed. SNORRI STURLUSON draws upon *HAUSTLONG*, a shield poem, or form of SKALDIC POETRY, for this tale.

**HRYM** The frost giant who stood at the helm of NAGLFAR, the ship made of dead men's nails, which headed toward the battlefields of RAGNAROK at the end of the world.

**HUGI** (Thought) The young giant who outran fleet-footed THIALFI, servant of the god THOR, at the court of UTGARD-LOKI. Hugi was, it turned out, the embodiment of thought, and no one can move faster than thought.

**HUGIN** (Thought) One of the god ODIN's two RAVENs. The other was MUNIN (Memory). Each morning Odin sent the two ravens to fly about the NINE WORLDS, then return to HLIDSKIALF, Odin's high seat. They would perch on his shoulders and tell him what they had seen.

**HUMANS** According to Norse mythology, the first humans were carved from trees by ODIN and his brothers VILI and VE (see "The First Humans," under CREATION). They cut down an ASH tree and from it made the first man, ASK. From an elm tree they carved the first woman, EMBLA. Then the three gods gave the first humans spirit and life, understanding and movement, speech, hearing, and sight.

These humans lived in or surrounded by MIDGARD, which was either the land in which they dwelled or the protective wall that surrounded the Earth. The souls of human warriors went to VALHALLA or SESSRUMNIR, the great halls of ODIN and FRIGG, respectively, where they lived until they were called upon to help the gods fight at RAGNAROK, the battle at the end of time.

Many of the surviving manuscripts of Norse mythology include attempts to give the gods human origins. Thirteenth-century writer SNORRI STURLUSON, for example, writes in his prologue to *GYLFAGINNING* that Odin was first a great leader from Asia who traveled north, settling his sons into kingships in the lands that would become SCANDINAVIA. Members of royal families also attempted to link their ancestry to the gods, often developing elaborate genealogies back to some of these stories and hiring poets to write SAGAs that would show how a human king was actually related to a god.

**HVERGELMIR** (Roaring Cauldron) The well or spring in NIFLHEIM from which gush the 11 rivers called the ELIVAGAR. The third root of the World Tree, YGGDRASIL, hangs over the poisonous vapor that rises from Hvergelmir. Nearby lives NITHOG, the corpse-eating dragon that nibbles on the roots of the sacred tree.

**HYMIR** (Dark One) A sea giant who owned a large cauldron that the gods wanted for brewing their ale. The gods TYR and THOR won the cauldron from Hymir and then killed him.

**HYNDLA** The giantess visited by the goddess FREYA, who asked Hyndla to reveal the lineage of her human lover, OTTAR. The story is told in the POETIC EDDA in *HYNDLULJOTH* (specifically, the *Lay of Hyndla*).

**HYNDLULJOTH** (*HYNDLULJOD*; *Lay of Hyndla*) A poem found in the POETIC EDDA. This poem was included in an Icelandic manuscript compiled in the late 14th century, but it was most likely written down in the 12th century.

*Hyndluljoth* contains many stories. One is of FREYA's visit to HYNDLA, who is apparently the bride of a giant, lives in a cave, and rides a WOLF. It also presents information on the main AESIR gods.

Part of this poem is known as the "Shorter Voluspa." *Hyndluljoth*, like the full *Voluspa*, perhaps the most important poem in the *Poetic Edda*, contains a question-and-answer session and tells a story of LOKI, the trickster god.

**HYROKKIN** The giantess who launched the longship HRINGHORNI, the funeral pyre of the slain god BALDER. She rode an enormous WOLF using serpents as reins. The BERSERKERS killed the wolf, but Hyrokkin pushed the ship into the water with her own strength.

# I

**ICELAND** An island nation in the Arctic and North Atlantic Oceans, about 570 miles west of NORWAY. Iceland is considered part of SCANDINAVIA and the Nordic nations, and as such it shares language and cultural histories with Norway, SWEDEN, and DENMARK. Norwegians settled this volcanic island in the middle of the ninth century A.D. The settlers took with them their old religion and the stories of the gods and goddesses of the NORSE. In their isolation, the peoples of this rugged land maintained their beliefs in the old gods longer than their relatives in Europe, who converted to Christianity in the 10th century. Iceland became a Christian land during the 11th century; however, for some reason unclear to modern historians and literary experts, the stories of the old Norse gods thrived in Iceland until well into the 13th century, long after they had faded from the cultures of Norway, Sweden, and Denmark.

Most of the surviving manuscripts about the mythology of the Norse were created by artists living in the ninth and 10th centuries and recorded by scribes living in Iceland in the 13th, 14th, and later centuries. The great stories in the *POETIC EDDA* were composed by anonymous poets and later written down by people skilled in the new art of writing and manuscript creation. These poems are part of the *CODEX REGIUS*, a manuscript written in the late 13th century and found in a farmhouse in Iceland in the 17th century. SNORRI STURLUSON, the author of the *PROSE EDDA*, was a scholar, historian, and chieftain in Iceland who wrote his works in the early 1200s in an effort to preserve the stories for later generations. He based his work on older poems and prose SAGAs, stories of heroes from Scandinavia that provide clues and details concerning the beliefs of these people. The language of these manuscripts,

known as Old Norse or Old Icelandic, is closely related to the modern languages of Scandinavia, particularly modern Icelandic.

Very little archaeological evidence of the beliefs in the AESIR and VANIR gods remains in Iceland, for it was settled late in the age of the Nordic people. While rock carvings and burial sites in Norway, Sweden, and Denmark from the Bronze Age (3500–1000 B.C.) and later provide scientists with additional evidence of the beliefs of these people, very few such carvings exist in Iceland.

**IDAVOLL** The plain or field in ASGARD where the shining palaces of the AESIR gods stood. It was here that the young gods played games such as chess, and it was here that the god BALDER was slain by his blind brother, HODUR. After RAGNAROK (the end of the world), Idavoll became green again at the Regeneration. New halls were built by the surviving gods. It is said that they found the golden chess pieces of their slaughtered friends and looked at them in wonder as they remembered the past.

**IDI** One of the storm giants, brother of THIAZZI and GANG and son of OLVALDI, who left piles of gold to be divided among his sons (see "Skade and Niord," under SKADE).

**IDUNN** (IDUNA) The golden haired goddess who supplied the AESIR gods with apples that gave them eternal youth. Idunn was the wife of BRAGI, the god of poetry.

She was probably an important goddess, but the only myth that survives about Idunn is the one in which she is kidnapped by the giant THIAZZI. In the *PROSE EDDA* SNORRI STURLUSON bases his retelling of the myth partially on the poem *HAUSTLONG*, by mid-nineth- to early-10th-century Norwegian poet Thiodor of Hvini.

**Idunn's Apples** The goddess Idunn supplied the gods with the apples that kept them forever young. One day Idunn and her apples were stolen away. According to Snorri, the great god ODIN, his brother HOENIR, and LOKI, the sly one, went exploring. When they became hungry they killed an ox, built a fire, and started to cook the meat. But no matter what they did, the meat remained raw and inedible.

A huge EAGLE landed on a tree nearby and said that he would make their fire burn like a furnace to cook the meat if only he could have a share of the food. The hungry travelers agreed to the bargain, the fire burned bright, the meat cooked, and the eagle ate almost all of it in a gulp.

Loki, quick to anger, swiped at the eagle but got carried away in its talons. The eagle dragged Loki over rocks and thorns until he begged for mercy. The eagle would not let Loki go until he promised to deliver to him Idunn and her apples of youth. Loki agreed at once and the eagle dropped him back to Earth. After Loki limped back to his companions, he did not tell them of his promise to the eagle, who he had realized was the giant Thiazzi in disguise.

Back in ASGARD, Loki wasted no time, for he was terrified of the fierce Thiazzi and knew he must somehow keep his promise. Loki ran to the peaceful orchard that Idunn tended with her husband, Bragi. He told her that he had found some apples in MIDGARD that looked just like hers. He urged her to bring her basket of apples and accompany him to Midgard, so that they might compare apples.

Sweet Idunn was glad to follow Loki. She would be very happy to find more apples for the gods to eat.

Idunn's magic apples promise eternal youth to the gods and goddesses. *(Historical Picture Service–Chicago)*

As soon as Idunn and Loki were across BIFROST, the RAINBOW BRIDGE, and into Midgard, the giant eagle swooped down, seized Idunn and carried her away. Once in THRYMHEIM, his fortress, Thiazzi shut the golden maiden in the highest tower.

Without the magic apples, the faces of the Aesir and ASYNJUR—the gods and goddesses—began to wrinkle and sag, their rosy cheeks faded, their hair grew white and thin, and their joints stiff and creaky, for these gods and goddesses were ancient. The gods and goddesses met to decide what to do. Everyone was there except Loki. The gods immediately concluded that Loki must have been up to some mischief. They searched for him and found him. Odin ordered Loki to bring back Idunn and her apples under threat to his life.

Loki fled in terror to the goddess FREYA to borrow her flying suit of FALCON feathers. With this, he flew off to Thrymheim. Fortunately for Loki, Thiazzi had gone fishing, and Idunn was unguarded. Loki used his magic to turn the maiden and her basket of apples into a small nut, which he grasped in his claws. Odin, the all-seeing, caught sight of the falcon from afar and saw that behind him came an enormous eagle—Thiazzi.

"Quickly build a pile of shavings and kindling at the gates of Asgard," Odin commanded.

Just in time, Loki flew over the walls of Asgard. The eagle was so close behind that he got caught in the flames that roared up when the dry kindling was lit. The eagle fell to the ground, and the gods slew him. Then Loki said the magic words, and Idunn stood before them once more, offering her wonderful apples with a happy smile.

It is of particular interest to mythologists that Loki turns Idunn into a nut. This symbol of eternal youth is often found in old Scandinavian burial sites. Idunn may have been a VANIR goddess of fertility, youth, and death. This is the only surviving myth about her.

**ING**  In Norse mythology Ing was a name associated with the god FREY, who was a god of the VANIR until he was sent to ASGARD as part of the exchange that ended the WAR BETWEEN THE AESIR AND THE VANIR. Ing was a term of respect that preceded Frey's name, as in Ingunar Frey, which is found in the surviving NORSE literature. Ing is also a hero of an Old English RUNE poem and the name of the Norse rune that represented the "ng" sound (see YNGVI). The word is a common element in many place-names in SCANDINAVIA.

Scholars suggest that Ing was a Germanic god or hero. One old tale tells of the wagon of Ing traveling eastward over the ocean waves. Some suggest that the wagon carried the Sun through the underworld during the night hours to return it to the east, where it would rise the next morning.

Other scholars suggest that Ing was a son of MANNUS, who was the first human in Old German mythology, a source of Norse mythology. Ing may have been a name of the Germanic people known as the Ingvaeones or Ingaevones.

**IRONWOOD**  The forest east of MIDGARD. In Ironwood lived the wicked witch whose children were werewolves, trolls, and the wolves SKOLL and HATI, who would devour the Sun and the Moon at the last battle, RAGNAROK.

# J

**JARNSAXA** (Ironstone)   One of the wives of the god THOR. She bore him two sons, MAGNI (Mighty) and MODI (Courage).

**JORD**   See FJORGYN (1).

**JORMUNGAND**   The giant serpent—also known as the Midgard Serpent, Midgard Snake, or Midgard Worm—offspring of LOKI and the ogress ANGRBODA. Jormungand is the brother of the WOLF FENRIR and HEL, the goddess of death.

The huge serpent was cast into the sea by ODIN and doomed to encircle the Earth, his tail in his mouth. Jormungand and THOR were mortal enemies. On one occasion Thor caught the serpent using an ox-head for bait, but the giant HYMIR snipped the line and the serpent disappeared beneath the waves. The serpent appeared again at RAGNAROK and made his way onto the land, spewing venom. Thor killed the serpent but was himself poisoned by the deadly venom.

**JOTUN**   The Scandinavian word for "giant." The GIANTS lived in JOTUNHEIM. The first giant was YMIR, formed at the beginning of time out of fire and ice, long before the first gods and humans. The first gods, ODIN, VILI, and VE, destroyed Ymir and created the world from his body (see CREATION). The giants were constantly at war with the gods of ASGARD. At the end of the world, or RAGNAROK, gods, giants, and monsters fought a final battle and nearly all died.

Giants were generally thought of as personifications of destructive forces, huge, ugly, and fierce. They had heads of stone and feet of ice. Many were known as HRIMTHURSSAR, or frost giants, and their names referred to frost, storms, snow, and ice, the scourges of northern winters. They could transform themselves into an EAGLE or WOLF; however, in many of the Norse myths they also assume shapes resembling those of normal people or gods.

Many of the giantesses were beautiful and more than friendly to the gods. The beautiful GERDA married the god FREY. The giantess GRID, friend of the great god ODIN, loaned THOR weapons to defend himself against the giant GEIRROD (1). HYROKKIN single-handedly pushed BALDER's ship, HRINGHORNI, into the sea at Balder's funeral. Thor married the giantess. JARNSAXA, who bore him two sons, MODI and MAGNI. SKADE, the daughter of the giant THIAZZI, married the Vanir god NIORD.

**JOTUNHEIM** (JOTUNNHEIMAR; Giant Land)   The mountainous, freezing lands of the JOTUN, or GIANTS. Many manuscripts of Norse myths use the plural form, Jotunnheimar, to refer to the lands of the giants. Some scholars suggest that people viewed the giants as living in places that surrounded the edges of the world of HUMANS. Others say that people saw Jotunheim as one single place, just as they regarded ASGARD, the realm of the gods, as one place.

One of the three huge roots of the World Tree, YGGDRASIL, reached into Jotunheim. The great thunder god, THOR, traveled often to Jotunheim to battle the giants.

# K

**KENNING** A poetic technique used most frequently by the NORSE writers of SKALDIC POETRY, who created their art from about A.D. 700 to 1100. Essentially a kenning is a type of metaphor, using a set of words to represent a common noun. For example, for *sword,* the poet might use the NAME of a famous sword such as DAINSLEIF, which means "Dain's heirloom." Or a poet might refer to gold as "Sif's hair," which would remind the audience of the myth of the golden hair the god LOKI had the DWARFS make after he cut off the locks of the goddess SIF, wife of THOR.

Many kennings contain names and objects important to Norse mythology and provide scholars with hints and clues of stories that have been lost over time. At the same time, however, kennings are often the only mention of a name, and modern scholars and students have no other information to understand the meaning of that kenning. Kennings at the very least provide experts with the understanding that much about Norse mythology is lost to modern audiences.

**KVASIR** (Spittle) A wise man who was created from the spit of the AESIR and the VANIR gods after their battle (see WAR BETWEEN THE AESIR AND THE VANIR). Kvasir walked the world spreading his great wisdom to any who asked for it. He was slain by two DWARFS, FJALAR (2) and GALAR, who mixed his blood with honey to make a powerful MEAD that inspired any who drank it to talk with wisdom and poetry (see "The Mead of Poetry," under ODIN).

In another story Kvasir was a Vanir god noted for his great wisdom. He went to live in ASGARD after the war between the gods, along with the Vanir NIORD, FREY, and FREYA.

The word *kvas* (or *quaso*) means "strong beer" in many parts of eastern Europe and Russia, and "crushed fruit" in Danish. In British English a similar word, *squash,* denotes a fruit drink.

# L

**LAEDING** The first of three chains with which the gods tried to muzzle and secure the dangerous WOLF FENRIR. Laeding and the second chain, DROMI, were made of ordinary metal, and Fenrir broke them easily. Only the magical third chain, GLEIPNER, was strong enough to hold the wolf. Fenrir remained chained until the time of RAGNAROK, the battle that brought an end to the world of the gods.

**LAERAD** The great tree around which ODIN's hall, VALHALLA, was built. The she-goat HEIDRUN, who produced an endless supply of MEAD for the gods and heroes, and the stag EIKTHYRNIR nibbled at its branches.

**LAEVATEINN** (Guileful Twig) The magic sword that the god LOKI forged beneath the gates of death using magic RUNES. Only this sword could kill the cock Vidofnir, who sat in the branches of YGGDRASIL, the World Tree.

**LANDVAETTIR** (Land Wights) Spirits that protected the land (that is, the soil or ground). According to stories, huge crowds of Landvaettir might inhabit a place. They were invisible to people unless someone looked very closely in the right light at the right time. A law in ICELAND prohibited ships with dragonhead carvings on their bows from coming toward shore in case the huge monsters frightened away the Landvaettir. These wights (creatures that are neither mortals nor gods) are similar to land ELVES, though more connected to the soil than to an area.

**LAUFEY** (Tree Island) A giantess and mother of LOKI, whose father, FARBAUTI, was also a giant. Some stories say Laufey gave birth to Loki when a light-ning bolt thrown by Farbauti struck her. Laufey apparently did not raise Loki, since Icelandic author SNORRI STURLUSON and others say that the trickster god was a foster brother of ODIN, the most powerful Norse god.

In *Sorlathattra,* a Norse SAGA more ancient than Snorri's 13th-century PROSE EDDA, Loki's mother is named Nal, which means "needle." In this story, his mother is slender and weak.

**LAY** A short lyric or narrative (storytelling) poem, especially one intended to be sung, usually by traveling minstrels. These minstrels thus kept alive ancient stories dealing with mythology, history, or legendary adventures. In Norse mythology many of the poems in the POETIC EDDA are lays, such as the *Lay of Thrym,* or THRYMSKVITHA.

**LIF** The man who with his wife, LIFTHRASIR, survived RAGNAROK and repeopled the earth. During the fearful holocaust they took shelter in HODDMIMIR'S WOOD, another name for the World Tree, YGGDRASIL. They were nourished by the morning dew. They emerged from the tree unhurt when they saw the new SUN shining. They had children and started a new life for humankind. The story appears in the VAFTHRUDTNISMAL.

**LIFTHRASIR** (Eager for Life) The woman, wife of LIF, who survived RAGNAROK and with Lif began to repeople the earth. Lif and Lifthrasir hid in the World Tree, YGGDRASIL, during the holocaust that caused the end of the world. The myth forms part of the VAFTHRUDNISMAL.

**LIT** The DWARF who suddenly appeared at BALDER's funeral and got in the way of THOR, who was consecrating the funeral pyre with his magic hammer, MJOLLNIR. Hot tempered as always and stricken with sorrow at Balder's death, Thor kicked Lit into the flames of the pyre. Lit gained immortality in mythology by being burned to ashes along with the god Balder and his wife, NANNA.

## LODDFAFNIR
A man from MIDGARD (Middle Earth), that is, a human. In the *Lay of Loddfafnir*, part of the poem HAVAMAL from the POETIC EDDA, Loddfafnir tells his fellow men many words of wisdom. He had somehow found his way to the URDARBRUNN, a sacred place, where he heard the words of the High One (ODIN). Loddfafnir recounted these words to fellow mortals. The words contained much good advice. For example, beware of a witch's sweet words, always carry food if you have to cross a mountain, cherish your friends and be loyal to them, stay away from evil people, doing good deeds will make you feel happy, hold to your promises, and respect the wisdom of the elderly. There were also words full of ancient superstitions, such as those for warding off the curses made by witches.

## LOFN
A minor goddess, counted by SNORRI STURLUSON among the main ASYNJUR, or goddesses of the AESIR. Lofn was portrayed as gentle and good. ODIN and FRIGG gave her permission to help people find love. In many ways Lofn served as a matchmaker. She might help young people tell each other of their love or fulfill the dreams of a man or woman whose love of another was not returned. Lofn means "praise" or "praised."

## LOFNHEID
One of two daughter of HREIDMAR, a farmer who receives from the gods gold in compensation for their killing of Hreidmar's son OTR. The other daughter is LYNGHEID. Though the story of Hreidmar is also told in the legendary VOLSUNGA SAGA, Lofnheid and her sister are named only in the poem *Reginsmal*, part of the POETIC EDDA. Another of Hreidmar's sons, FAFNIR, kills his father as his sisters look on. Their father begs his daughters for help, but they declare themselves powerless against their brother. REGIN is their third brother.

## LOGI
(Flame) The young giant who defeated the trickster god, LOKI, in an eating contest at the court of the giant UTGARD-LOKI. It turned out that Logi was the embodiment of fire, which can consume anything and everything with great rapidity.

(See also "Thor's Journey to Utgard," under THOR.)

## LOKASENNA
A poem in the POETIC EDDA, part of the CODEX REGIUS. It consists of a "war of words" between LOKI and the other gods and goddesses.

## LOKI
Loki is known as the trickster god, the mischief maker, the father of lies and deceit, and the shape changer. He is the personification of both aspects of fire: the merry but potentially dangerous hearth fire and the destructive fire of forest and volcano.

Loki was the son of the giant FARBAUTI and of the giantess LAUFEY or Nal. He had two wives. The first was the fearful ogress ANGRBODA, with whom he had three monstrous offspring: HEL, the goddess of death and the underworld; JORMUNGAND, the Midgard Serpent who encircled the world; and FENRIR the wolf. His wife in ASGARD was SIGYN, with whom he had two sons, NARFI and VALI (1).

Loki was counted among the AESIR gods, but he was not one of them, as he was born among the JOTUN, the gods' enemies. Some say that he and the great god ODIN were blood brothers, which is why none of the gods dared to harm Loki, no matter how mischievous and malevolent he became.

Loki was handsome and could be amusing. He made the goddess SKADE laugh even while she mourned for her father, THIAZZI. Loki was sometimes helpful to the gods, for he was quick witted and always had an answer for everything, but often the gods would regret taking his advice.

It was Loki who accompanied THOR to JOTUNHEIM to retrieve Thor's magic hammer. Loki also thought of a way to outwit the giant who built Asgard's wall (see GIANT MASTER BUILDER). However, his solution was nothing but fraud and resulted in Thor committing murder within Asgard; such behavior was against the code of the Aesir.

Loki stole FREYA's necklace and cut off SIF's golden hair, yet it was he who went down to the underground caves of the DWARFS and brought back wonderful treasures for the gods (see TREASURES OF

Loki had three monstrous children: Fenrir, the wolf; Jormungand, the Midgard Serpent; and Hel, queen of the underworld. *(Anthony Mercatante)*

THE DWARFS). Loki double-crossed both the giant Thiazzi and the Aesir when he delivered IDUNN and her apples to the giant and then, disguised as a FALCON, carried Idunn back to Asgard, leading Thiazzi to his death.

Not only could Loki change himself into other creatures at will, such as a seal, a salmon, a fly, a falcon; he could also change his sex. As a mare, he was the mother of SLEIPNIR, Odin's eight-legged steed. He became an old crone when he tricked FRIGG into telling him that MISTLETOE was the only object on earth that could harm the gentle god BALDER. Even though Loki was the principal cause of Balder's death, the Aesir took no action against him.

However, when Loki came to AEGIR's banquet and flung vicious insults at all the gods and goddesses, the Aesir finally decided to punish the evil creature that Loki had become. At RAGNAROK (the day of doom), Loki led the forces of evil against the gods, and he and HEIMDALL killed each other.

**Loki's Mocking** Loki could be playful and charming, but as time went on, he became sinister, evil, and bad tempered. The story of Loki's mocking of the gods and goddesses, part of the LOKASENNA in the POETIC EDDA, shows Loki at his worst.

Aegir, the Jotun lord of the sea, invited the gods to a banquet in his coral caves under the island of HLESEY. He brewed the ale in the huge cauldron that Thor and TYR had taken from the giant HYMIR.

It was soon after the death of BALDER and the gods were subdued, talking quietly among themselves. Loki listened impatiently as they praised Aegir's servants, FIMAFENG and ELDIR. Suddenly Loki sprang up and stabbed Fimafeng with his knife, then fled. He soon returned, and this time his targets were the gods and goddesses and his weapons were poisonous words.

He insulted BRAGI, the god of poetry, by calling him a soft coward. One by one he accused each of the goddesses, Idunn, GEFION, Frigg, FREYA, and SIF, of being deceitful and unvirtuous. He laughed at NIORD for being a hostage from the VANIR gods and at Tyr for losing his hand in the jaws of the wolf Fenrir. No one escaped, not even FREY's servants, BYGGVIR and his wife BEYLA, nor HEIMDALL, who was mocked as being a mere servant of the gods. Even the great god Odin did not escape Loki's evil tongue. Loki sneered at him for once having turned himself into a witch, "a woman through and through."

At last Thor, who had been absent, entered the hall. His eyes glowed with rage, and his whiskers bristled when he heard Loki's vicious insults. He threatened to kill Loki there and then with his hammer, and Loki swiftly left.

**The Pursuit of Loki-Salmon**  After Loki insulted the gods and goddesses at a feast given by Aegir, the sea god, he fled from the wrath of the gods and built himself a hut in the mountains. The hut had doors on all four sides so that Loki could escape easily, for he knew that the gods wanted to punish him for his evil words and also for the death of the gentle god Balder.

By day Loki the SHAPE-SHIFTER turned himself into a salmon and swam in the mountain torrent at Franang's Falls. To distract himself in the evening, he fashioned a fine net—some say, the first fishing net. (In other poems the sea ogress RAN, Aegir's wife, invented the fishing net to catch drowning sailors and bring them to her domain under the waves.)

From his high seat, HLIDSKJALF, Odin could see far and wide over all NINE WORLDS. When he finally saw where Loki was hiding and in what guise, Odin went with a party of gods to capture the trouble-maker. Loki saw them coming and quickly threw the fishing net into the fire, then sprinted down to the stream and leapt in as a salmon.

The gods entered the hut and saw the remains of the net. KVASIR, a very wise god, concluded that a finished net might be very useful to the gods for catching slippery Loki-Salmon. The gods sat up all

Loki mocks the gods and goddesses with poisonous words at Aegir's feast. *(New York Public Library Picture Collection)*

A serpent drips venom onto the face of Loki, whom the gods have bound to a rock. *(Anthony Mercatante)*

night repairing and completing the net. At dawn they set out to catch Loki.

Loki escaped their clutches for quite a while, as they used the net to drag the stream, but in the end Thor caught him in midair as he made a flying leap over the net. To this day, the salmon is noted for its slender tail, a reminder, Northmen say, of how strongly Thor had held Loki in his powerful hand.

**Loki's Punishment** After the gods captured Loki, they dragged him into a dark cave. They changed Loki's son Vali into a WOLF who immediately attacked his brother Narfi and killed him. The gods took Narfi's intestines and bound Loki with

them. Once Loki was firmly bound, they changed the horrid bonds into iron. Then the icy goddess Skade placed a serpent over Loki's upturned face so that its venom would drip onto him.

Only Sigyn, Loki's faithful wife, stayed with Loki in the miserable cave. She held a bowl to catch the drops of venom, but when she turned aside to empty the poison, the drops fell on Loki's twisted face. He writhed with pain and terror, causing the Earth to tremble and quake. So Loki, the Norse myths say, is the cause of the earthquakes that terrify us.

Loki remained a prisoner until RAGNAROK, when he took his revenge on the gods, and they on him.

**LORA (LORRIDE)** Daughter of THOR and SIF and sister of THRUD (1).

**LOTHUR (LODUR)** According to the *VOLUSPA*, part of the *POETIC EDDA*, one of the three original AESIR gods who, along with his brothers ODIN and HOENIR created the world (see "The First Humans," under CREATION). In his *PROSE EDDA*, SNORRI STURLUSON identifies Lothur as VE and Hoenir as VILI.

Some mythologists have tried to identify Lothur with LOKI, but virtually nothing is known about this god.

**LYNGHEID** A daughter of the farmer HREIDMAR. Lyngheid looked on with her sister, LOFNHEID, as their brother FAFNIR killed their father for the hoard of gold he protected. The gods had given the gold to Hreidmar as compensation for their killing OTR, another son of Hreidmar. Lyngheid and her sister are mentioned only in *Reginsmal*, part of the *POETIC EDDA*, though the story of Otr and Hreidmar is also told in the legendary *VOLSUNGA SAGA*.

**LYNGVI (Heathery)** The island in the middle of the lake AMSVARTNIR (Red-Black) where ODIN and the gods bound the WOLF FENRIR. On Lyngvi, Fenrir waited for RAGNAROK, the battle at the end of time, when he would be freed to fight on the side of the giants.

# M

**MAGNI** (Mighty)   One of the two sons of the god THOR and the giantess JARNSAXA. His brother is MODI. At an early age Magni was strong enough to rescue his father from under the leg of the giant HRUNGNIR. As a reward Thor gave him the magnificent horse GULLFAXI, which had belonged to the giant. Magni was one of the seven AESIR who survived RAGNAROK, the end of the world, and inherited, with his brother, Thor's hammer, MJOLLNIR.

**MANAGARM** (Moon Dog)   A name used by 13th-century Icelandic historian SNORRI STURLUSON for one of the horrible wolves that destroy the SUN AND MOON at the time of RAGNAROK. The other WOLF was SKOLL. Managarm was also known as HATI. Managarm was one of the many sons of an old giantess, all of whom were wolves.

See also IRONWOOD.

**MANI**   The man who drove the chariot that carried the Moon across the sky. He is the son of MUNDILFARI and the brother of SOL. For company, Mani stole two children from MIDGARD (Middle Earth). Their names were BIL AND YUKI (Waning and Waxing). Some say that on a clear night the children in the Moon can be seen as dark shapes on the Moon's face, as they eternally carry a pail of water on a pole (see "Sun and Moon," under CREATION). At RAGNAROK, the WOLF HATI, which pursues the chariot across the skies, will devour the Moon.

**MANNUS**   The first HUMAN according to the stories of Old Germanic mythology, which influenced the development of Norse mythology. He was the son of Tuisto, a mythical figure about whom little is known today. Tuisto may have been a hybrid creature capable of giving birth to his own children, much like the first ancestor of the Norse gods, BURI. Mannus, however, is said to be human, while Buri's exact nature is unclear in the surviving Norse sources.

Mannus was the father of three human sons, who in turn were the fathers of the three Germanic tribes, the Ingvaeones (see ING), the Herminones, and the Istvaeones (or Iscaevones or Istraeones), all of which became important in the stories of Norse mythology. Some scholars suggest that these sons were godlike heroes rather than humans.

**MEAD**   An alcoholic drink made by fermenting honey and water. The creators of the Norse myths considered mead superior to the usual beer and ale (made by fermenting cereals flavored with hops) drunk by ordinary people. In VALHALLA mead was supplied in a never-ending flow by the she-GOAT HEIDRUN, and the gods and heroes never lacked the heavenly brew.

See also "The Mead of Poetry," under ODIN.

**MEGINGJARDIR** (MEGINGJORD, MEGINGIORD, MEGINGARDER; Power Belt)   The name SNORRI STURLUSON gave to the god THOR's magic belt. When the thunder god fastens it on, his already great powers become twice as strong. Megingjardir was one of three of Thor's great treasures, which included his mighty hammer, MJOLLNIR, and iron gloves. The belt is described in older Norse sagas, but only Snorri calls it Megingjardir.

**MENGLOD** (MENGLOTH; Necklace-Happy)   A very beautiful giantess who was served by eight maiden goddesses, including EIR. SVIPDAG fell in love with Menglod and traveled to the underworld to learn from his dead mother how to win the love of this maiden.

**MIDGARD** (Middle Earth) The world of HU-MANS. It was midway between ASGARD, the home of the gods, and JOTUNHEIM, the home of the GIANTS. Midgard was connected to Asgard by BIFROST, the RAINBOW BRIDGE. It was surrounded by an ocean in which lived JORMUNGAND, the Midgard Serpent. The first man and woman to live in Midgard were ASK and EMBLA. One of the three roots of the sacred tree, YGGDRASIL, was embedded in Midgard. Midgard was formed from the body of the giant YMIR.

**MIDSUMMER EVE** In northern countries, June 21, the longest day of the year in the Northern Hemisphere, was BALDER's Day, celebrated with bonfires and the observance of the sunset and sunrise. In many countries it was the custom to gather MISTLE-TOE on this day. Scientifically, it is the day of the summer SOLSTICE.

**MIMIR** In one myth Mimir is a wise god sent by the AESIR to the VANIR after the war between the two races of gods (see WAR BETWEEN THE AESIR AND THE VANIR). Along with Mimir went HOENIR, who was rather slow witted. The Vanir were annoyed with Hoenir, and with the Aesir for having sent him, but did not dare harm him, for he was ODIN's brother. Instead they cut off Mimir's head and sent it to Odin. Odin used his magic to preserve the head, which from then on imparted its wisdom when Odin came to seek counsel of it.

Another myth says that Odin sacrificed one of his eyes to Mimir, the guardian of the well of knowledge. Mimir granted Odin permission to drink from the well to gain wisdom and poetic inspiration.

**MIMIR'S WELL** The well of wisdom under the second root of the tree YGGDRASIL in JOTUNHEIM. The head of MIMIR resides beside the well. The god ODIN visited the well seeking wisdom. HEIMDALL, the WATCHMAN OF THE GODS, left his horn there until he needed it to announce RAGNAROK, the end of the world.

**MISTLETOE** A European plant (*Viscum album*) that grows as a parasite on trees. In Norse mythology it is known as the sprig that was hurled at the god BALDER by his blind brother, HODUR. Because mistle-

A sprig of mistletoe killed the god Balder. *(New York Public Library Picture Collection)*

toe has weak stems, some scholars suggest that the trickster god, LOKI, used his magic arts on the mistletoe to make it strong and sharp enough to kill Balder.

**MJOLLNIR** The hammer of the god THOR. It was made by the DWARFS BROKK and EITRI. The hammer was a symbol of Thor's strength and of the thunderbolt he personified.

The hammer had a massive head and a short handle and was shaped somewhat like a cross. The TREASURES OF THE DWARFS tells the reason for its peculiar shape. While Eitri was shaping the hammer in the foundry, LOKI, who had changed himself into a gadfly, pestered Brokk, who worked the bellows for his brother. At a crucial point in the making of the hammer, Loki stung Brokk on his eyelid; the dwarf was distracted and let go of the bellows. The fire died and Eitri did not have enough heat to finish the handle. For many centuries Norsemen wore the hammer's likeness as an amulet. Many of these amulets have been discovered in archaeological digs in SCANDI-NAVIA and England. Many ancient gravestones and rune stones also depict Thor's hammer.

The gods considered Mjollnir to be their greatest treasure, for it alone could be used to defend ASGARD against the GIANTS. When Thor hurled it, it always struck its mark and returned instantly into his hand, like a boomerang. Although mighty in size, it could be magically shrunk to fit inside Thor's shirt.

The hammer was a symbol of fertility. In "The Theft of Thor's Hammer," Thor dressed himself as a bride when he went to visit the giant THRYM, who had stolen the hammer. Thor knew that at some point in the wedding ceremony a hammer was always placed in the lap of the bride, for such was the custom of the Norse. When Thrym placed Mjollnir in Thor's lap, Thor retrieved his hammer.

Mjollnir was also a symbol of resurrection. In "Thor's Journey to Utgard," when Thor waves Mjollnir over the skin and bones of his dead goats, the goats spring back to life.

Mjollnir was used at funerals as well. When BALDER lay on his funeral pyre, Thor consecrated the funeral with his hammer.

With Mjollnir, Thor killed the giant HRUNGNIR and also the GIANT MASTER BUILDER, who built Asgard's wall.

The only time that the hammer seemed to be ineffectual was when Thor struck the giant SKRYMIR with it. Skrymir said that he thought he was being assaulted by delicate leaves and twigs. However, it turned out that the hammer had made huge dents in a hillside instead of in Skrymir's head, thanks to the giant's clever magic.

After RAGNAROK, the end of the world, Thor's sons, MAGNI and MODI, inherited Mjollnir.

## MODGUD
The keeper of GIALLARBRU, the bridge over the GIOLL (2) River on the way to the underworld. HEL challenged the god HERMOD, who was searching for his slain brother, BALDER. Modgud told Hermod that Balder was in NIFLHEIM and told him how to get there.

## MODI
(Courage) One of the two sons of the god THOR and the giantess JARNSAXA. Along with his brother, MAGNI, Modi was one of the seven AESIR gods to survive RAGNAROK. He and Magni inherited Thor's hammer, MJOLLNIR.

## MOKKURKALFI
(Mist Calf) The clay monster made by the JOTUNS as a second, or substitute, for HRUNGNIR in his duel with the god THOR. Mokkurkalfi was nine leagues tall, or about nine miles. The Jotuns equipped Mokkurkalfi with the heart of a mare. Thor's servant, THIALFI, hacked the clay figure to pieces.

## MOON
See CREATION; SUN AND MOON.

## MUNDILFARI
(Turner) A man from MIDGARD who named his daughter SOL (Sun) and his son MANI (Moon). The gods were outraged that a HUMAN should have the nerve to call his children after the Sun and the Moon. They stole the children and set them to driving the chariots of the Sun and the Moon eternally through the heavens (see "Sun and Moon," under CREATION; SUN AND MOON).

## MUNIN
(Memory) One of the god ODIN's two RAVENs. The other was HUGIN (Thought). Each morning Odin sent the two ravens to fly about the NINE WORLDS. Then they returned to HLIDSKIALF, Odin's high seat, perched on his shoulders, and told him what they had seen.

## MUSPELL
A group of people or creatures from the fiery lands of MUSPELLHEIM who would ride their horses against the gods at RAGNAROK, the battle at the end of time. SNORRI STURLUSON tells of "the sons of Muspell" and "the people of Muspell" in the PROSE EDDA. He also says that NAGLFAR is Muspell's ship.

The fact that the name Muspell is also used to refer to the same groups in some works of the POETIC EDDA suggests to modern experts that Muspell was an important figure in ancient Norse myths. Some say Muspell was apparently a giant that ruled over a vast world of evil creatures. He may have ruled a land of heat and flame and thrown fire as his weapon in battle. Surviving stories do not contain enough information to answer these questions.

Muspell's sons are many—enough to form a vast army or a horde of warriors at the end battle between the gods and giants. They fight with the weapons of the land in which they lived: fire, light, and heat.

In the early 20th century, scholars believed Muspell referred to a place, and that that place was named after this very old mythical giant.

**MUSPELLHEIM** (Home of Destruction)  The realm of fire. Heat from MUSPELL's fires and ice from NIFLHEIM helped to form the first living beings at the CREATION of the world.

Muspellheim was ruled over by the fire giant, SURT, who guarded it with a flaming sword. At RAGNAROK, the end of the world, Surt burst through a crack in the dome of the sky and destroyed the world by fire. The forces of evil that fought the gods at Ragnarok are called the sons of Muspell.

# N

**NABBI** One of the two DWARFS who fashioned FREYA's gold-bristled boar, HILDISVINI. The other was DAIN (1).

**NAGLFAR** (Conveyance Made of Nails) The ship made from dead men's nails. It carried the GIANTS into battle against the gods at RAGNAROK. *Naglfar*'s size would depend on how many men had been buried with unpared fingernails. According to SNORRI STURLUSON, an ancient superstition said that the nails of the dead must be cut to keep the size of the fatal ship small and thus give the gods a better chance in battle.

**NAGLFARI** (Darkling) A giant, the first husband of NOTT (Night). They had a son named AUD. The only information about this giant comes from the stories of 13th-century Icelandic poet SNORRI STURLUSON in *GYLFAGINNING*.

**NAMES** Norse mythology is rich with meaningful names. Gods may have dozens of names; the supreme god ODIN, for example, was known by more than 150 names or titles. Each character, whether human or supernatural, received his or her own name and often many different names. In Norse poetry, swords, chains, wells, animals, and even bridges received names.

Many names of the gods, DWARFS, and GIANTS reflect what scholars see as a strong tradition among the NORSE to give significant names to the objects of mythology. Scholars, however, suggest that some of the names in the manuscripts that have survived to modern times reflect a tendency among some editors and scribes of the stories to poke fun at the Norse tradition of naming objects.

**NANNA** AESIR goddess, wife of BALDER and mother of FORSETI. After Balder's death Nanna died of grief, and the gods placed her on his funeral pyre to burn with him. She accompanied Balder to NIFLHEIM, the realm of HEL, and gave gifts to HERMOD for him to take back to ASGARD.

**NARFI** (NARI) The son of LOKI and SIGYN and the brother of VALI (1). Narfi was killed by his brother, who was turned into a WOLF. His entrails are used to bind Loki to the rocks of an underground cave (see "Loki's Punishment," under LOKI).

**NASTROND** (Strand of Corpses) The gruesome shore in HEL's underworld where the corpses of the evil dead washed up and where the dragon NITHOG feasted. After RAGNAROK (the end of the world) there was still a Nastrond and a Nithog to feed upon the bodies of the dead.

**NERTHUS** (HERTHA; Earth) A north German goddess, an EARTH MOTHER, worshiped as a goddess of fertility. Some say that she was the sister-wife of the god NIORD and the mother of FREY and FREYA. The Roman historian Tacitus wrote that when Nerthus appeared in her wagon, drawn by oxen, it was a cause for rejoicing throughout the land, and sacrifices were made in her honor.

**NIDAFJOLL** (Dark Mountains) Two interpretations for this name exist in Norse poetry. One is a mountain range in the underworld, a place from which the dragon NITHOG flew, carrying corpses in his claws.

The other interpretation, from the works of SNORRI STURLUSON, is that Nidafjoll was the shining land that survived the devastation of RAGNAROK, the final battle between the AESIR gods and the GIANTS. In this land stood the magnificent hall known as SINDRI. The righteous people who survived the conflict would dwell in Nidafjoll, a new world.

## NIDAVELLIR (Dark Crags)

The home of the DWARFS. Not much is known about the location of Nidavellir in the NINE WORLDS. It may have been an area within SVARTALFHEIM, the home of the dark elves.

## NIFLHEIM (World of Fog)

A vast waste of frozen fog, brutal cold, and endless night. Niflheim was the lowest region of the underworld. From its poisonous fountain, HVERGELMIR, flowed 11 ice-cold rivers, the ELIVAGIR. The rivers poured into the huge chasm, GINUNGAGAP, and froze. Fiery clouds from MUSPELLHEIM melted the ice and turned it into mist. From the whirling mist and fire came the first giant, YMIR (see CREATION).

The goddess HEL ruled over this land of the dead. Niflheim was the home of the dragon NITHOG and other serpents. They nibbled on one of the roots of the World Tree, YGGDRASIL, that reached into the underworld.

After MIDGARD (Middle Earth) was created, the gods pushed Niflheim deep into the ground so that its terrible cold would not freeze the Earth.

## NINE WORLDS

In Norse mythology the Nine Worlds were broken into three levels.

- At the top level were ASGARD, the home of the AESIR; VANAHEIM, the home of the VANIR; and Alfheim, the home of the light ELVES.
- At the middle level, and connected to Asgard by BIFROST, the RAINBOW BRIDGE, were MIDGARD (Middle Earth), the home of HUMANS; JOTUNHEIM, the home of the JOTUNS, or GIANTS; and SVARTALFHEIM, the home of the dark elves.
- In the underworld were NIFLHEIM, world of the dead, cold, and misty, whose citadel was Hel, home of HEL, queen of the dead; and MUSPELL-HEIM, world of fire, presided over by the fire god, SURT.

In some tellings of the myths there was also NIDAVELLIR at the middle level; it was cited as the home of the DWARFS and may have been part of Svartalfheim.

The World Tree, YGGDRASIL, connected all Nine Worlds.

From his high seat, HLIDSKIALF, the great god ODIN could see what was happening in all Nine Worlds with the help of his ravens HUGIN and MUNIN. (See also RAVEN.)

## NIORD (NJORD)

The Norse god of the sea and seafarers, and also a fertility god. Niord was a VANIR god. He went to live in ASGARD after the WAR BETWEEN THE AESIR AND THE VANIR. He took with him his twin children, FREY and FREYA, both fertility gods. In some tellings Niord's first wife, and the mother of the twins, was NERTHUS, his sister. As the AESIR did not approve of marriage between brother and sister, Niord had to leave Nerthus behind. According to SNORRI STURLUSON, Niord's second wife was SKADE, goddess and giantess of winter. Niord's home was NOATUN, a bustling shipyard, noisy with the sound of the wind and the sea and the seabirds. Skade and Niord could not live happily together, for Skade hated the cheerful shipyard, while Niord felt unhappy at Skade's grim, cold mountain home. After spending nine nights together in each other's lands, the two decided to live apart.

## NITHOG (NIDHUG; Corpse Tearer)

The DRAGON that lived in NIFLHEIM at the foot of the World Tree, YGGDRASIL, and gnawed at its roots. The squirrel RATATOSK brought gossipy messages between the EAGLE at the top of the tree and the dragon at the roots. As well as feeding upon the roots of the sacred tree, Nithog fed on the corpses washed down from NASTROND into the bubbling cauldron of HVERGELMIR. At RAGNAROK, the end of the world, Nithog would harvest many corpses and survive to live in the new world.

**NOATUN** (Ship Haven) Hall of the VANIR god NIORD when he came to live in ASGARD. It was on the seashore. Niord, god of seafarers, loved the sound of the waves and the seabirds and the noises of the shipyard, but his wife SKADE did not.

**NORDI** (North) One of the four DWARFS who held up the sky. The other three are SUDRI (South), AUSTRI (East), and VESTRI (West). These dwarfs are named in early Norse poetry, but only 13th-century Icelandic poet SNORRI STURLUSON assigned Nordi and his three companions the job of holding up the four corners of the sky.

**NORFI** A giant, the father of NOTT. Norfi was one of the first giants in JOTUNHEIM.

**NORNS** (NORNIR; Fates) The three spirits of destiny who spun a thread of life for every living being, including gods, men, giants, and DWARFS. They shaped the life of each one from the first day to the last.

The three sisters lived near the URDARBRUNN (Well of Urd) at the foot of the World Tree, YGGDRASIL. Each day they watered the roots of Yggdrasil with the well's sacred water.

The names of the three sisters were URD (Past), VERDANDE (Present), and SKULD (Future). Urd is the oldest of the sisters; often she is pictured as looking backward. Verdande looks straight before her. Skuld usually wears a mysterious veil and carries a scroll in her hands.

The three sisters were more powerful than the gods, for the thread they spun was the destiny of the universe. They measured time and controlled it, and the gods were helpless against them. The gods held all their important meetings by the Well of Urd, a sacred place to them.

In northern folklore the Norns sometimes appear as spinners, and the spider is therefore associated with them.

The Norns are mentioned in both the *PROSE EDDA* and the *POETIC EDDA*.

**NORSE** The name of a specific language group and the people who spoke the languages in that group. Old Norse is a dead language; no group of people speaks it today as their first language. It is part of the North Germanic group of languages in the Indo-European language family; this group is also known as the Norse, or Scandinavian, languages. Old Norse is related to modern Danish, Norwegian, Swedish, Icelandic, and Faeroese, the language of the Faeroe Islands. Most of the surviving manuscripts of the mythology of SCANDINAVIA, such as the *CODEX REGIUS*, were written in Old Norse.

*Norse* also refers to ancient peoples who lived in the region of northwest Europe known as Scandinavia, particularly those who spoke Old Norse or one of its dialects. One group of Norse people were known as Norsemen or VIKINGS.

**NORWAY** One of the three principal nations of SCANDINAVIA, Norway occupies the western side of the Scandinavian peninsula in northwestern Europe. People have made this land their home since the last great ice age ended more than 13,000 years ago.

Norway features many archaeological sites to provide evidence of the worship of the Norse gods. Bronze Age rock carvings near Kalnes, Norway, show men in boats and sun images. At least three burial ships from the VIKING age (about A.D. 800–1000) have been uncovered near Oslo. The Oseberg ship, considered the oldest Viking ship yet found, was built between 850 and 900. It was buried for about 1,000 years and discovered by archaeologists in the early 1900s. The boat itself was elaborately carved. It contained small wagons for carrying "gods," an ornately decorated sleigh or sled, and a narrow tapestry portraying scenes from mythology. An elaborate bucket onboard contained APPLEs, a symbol of fertility. Many of these artifacts are on display in museums in Oslo. Churches in Hallingdal and Hegge, meanwhile, contain evidence of the "gods," including carvings that experts believe are representations of ODIN.

Some of Norway's contributions to NORSE history and literature are actually preserved in the manuscripts from ICELAND. The SAGAS, lays, and poems found in Iceland tell of Norway's kings and warrior heroes. Few manuscripts of the Norse age have actually been found in Norway itself.

Ships were important to the ancient Norse people, not only as a means of transportation, but also as a symbol of the voyage from life to death. Shown here is the Oseberg ship, the oldest known Viking ship to survive to the present day. (©University Museum of Cultural Heritage—University of Oslo, Norway; photographer unknown)

**NOTT** (Night) The dark-haired daughter of NORFI, one of the first giants of JOTUNHEIM. She married three times. Her first husband was NAGLFARI (Darkling); their son was AUD. Her second husband was ANNAR (Another); their daughter was Earth.

Her third husband was DELLING (Dawn); their son was DAG (Day).

The gods gave Nott and her son Dag each a chariot to ride through the heavens (see "Night and Day," under CREATION). Nott's lead horse was HRIMFAXI.

**OAK** The largest tree of the forests that covered northern Europe, the oak was sacred to THOR, god of thunder and lightning, and a symbol of strength and endurance. There were no great oaks in Iceland, but early settlers from the Norse lands brought oak pillars with them and set up shrines to Thor. Early Christian missionaries such as Boniface (eighth century) considered it their duty to destroy oak trees and groves where the pagan gods had been worshiped.

**OD** (ODUR) The husband of FREYA and father of HNOSSA. Od left Freya to roam the Earth; it is said that Freya wept golden tears for her lost husband. Some scholars think that Od may have been the god ODIN in one of his many guises.

**ODIN** Chief of the AESIR gods. The god of war and death, as well as a sky god and the god of wisdom and poetry. Odin is sometimes called ALFODR, the father of the gods.

He was descended from one of the earliest gods, BOR, and the giantess BESTLA. His brothers were VILI and VE (also called HOENIR and LOTHUR, respectively). (See CREATION.) Odin's Aesir wife was FRIGG. His sons included THOR, VALI, and possibly TYR. Odin had many other wives and children.

Odin's hall in ASGARD was VALASKIALF. From his throne, HLIDSKIALF, in the hall's high tower, Odin could survey all NINE WORLDS.

His RAVENs, HUGIN and MUNIN, brought Odin news. He gave his food to his two wolves GERI and FREKI (see WOLF), for Odin needed nothing but the sacred MEAD for nourishment. Odin's eight-legged steed was called SLEIPNIR.

GUNGNIR was Odin's spear. On his arm Odin wore the marvelous ring DRAUPNIR, from which dropped eight other rings every nine nights. When he rode into battle he wore an EAGLE helmet and armor. When he wandered peacefully on Earth (as he often did), Odin wore a sky-blue cape and a broad-brimmed hat.

Odin had only one eye, for he gave his other eye to MIMIR in exchange for wisdom. Odin could compose poetry, for he had drunk the MEAD of poetry.

Odin was also thought of as a magician, for he knew the secrets of the RUNES (the earliest alphabet used by the Norse), which he had obtained by hanging himself from the World Tree, YGGDRASIL. For this reason he is sometimes called Lord of the Gallows (see below).

Odin had another palace, named VALHALLA, where he entertained heroes who had fallen in battle and who would help him fight the frost giants (HRIMTHURSSAR) at RAGNAROK, the end of the world. But Odin and most of his warriors would be killed at Ragnarok; Odin, by the monster-wolf, FENRIR. Many wonderful tales are told about Odin, the greatest of the gods. He had as many as 200 different NAMES and attributes.

Odin, along with Thor, FREY, and Tyr, was worshiped for many years after the coming of Christianity to northern Europe.

**Lord of the Gallows** Odin was called Lord of the Gallows, God of the Hanged, and God of the Spear, among many other names. Odin was the god of knowledge but paid dearly for his wisdom. In one poem (HAVAMAL, or *Words of the High One*), Odin hanged himself from the branches of Yggdrasil, the sacred tree. He wounded himself with his spear and hung there for nine days and nine nights, without nourishment. At the end of that time he came back to life and picked up the magic runes that had dropped from the tree. The runes brought secret

This carved stone from Gotland, Sweden, shows Odin on his eight-legged steed, Sleipnir, and warriors aboard a Viking longship. *(New York Public Library Picture Collection)*

knowledge to Odin. He passed on this wisdom to both gods and humans.

In later years men would make human sacrifices to Odin by hanging prisoners and victims on gallows. It was said that Odin and his ravens would visit the victims and talk to them.

**The Mead of Poetry** The mead of poetry was the wondrous liquid created by the gods after the WAR BETWEEN THE AESIR AND THE VANIR. Whoever drank the mead would acquire wisdom and the inspiration to make poetry.

After the truce between the two races of gods (the Aesir and the VANIR), each god and goddess spat into a great jar to put a seal on their friendship. According to a myth in the PROSE EDDA and *Havamal* in the POETIC EDDA, the Aesir then carried off the jar, and out of the spittle they fashioned a man, KVASIR, who walked the world spreading great wisdom to all who asked for it.

The wicked DWARFS FJALAR (2) and GALAR killed Kvasir, collected his blood in three vats, and mixed it with honey to make a powerful mead, which they shared with no one. One day, in a fit of rage, the dwarfs murdered the giant GILLING and his wife. They were forced to give the mead to Gilling's angry son, SUTTUNG, in exchange for their lives.

Suttung built a strong underground cave in the mountain HNITBORG, where he lived. There he placed the three containers of mead and entrusted his daughter, GUNLOD, to guard them.

Because Suttung was a boastful, bragging kind of giant, it was not long before the Aesir heard what had happened to the divine mead. Odin, a master of disguise, turned himself into a giant of a man and went to JOTUNHEIM, calling himself BOLVERK. There, he sharpened the scythes of nine slaves who were at work in the fields owned by the giant BAUGI, Suttung's brother. The slaves managed to kill one another with their carefully honed scythes.

As Baugi now had no fieldhands, he agreed to let Odin-Bolverk work for him, for the one-eyed man looked very strong and seemed to need no rest. Odin put his magic to use. He worked better than nine men, for Baugi had promised to try to persuade his brother to allow Odin a sip of the famous mead as a reward for his work.

When the work was done, Baugi talked to his brother, but of course Suttung refused to part with even one drop of mead. Baugi then drilled a hole into the mountain with the auger RATI, and Odin quickly turned himself into a slender serpent and squirmed his way into the chamber where Gunlod guarded the treasure.

When lonely Gunlod saw Odin, once more in the shape of a tall, handsome man, she forgot all the promises she had made to her father and entertained Odin for three days and three nights. At the end, she even offered Odin a sip of the precious mead from each of the three containers, BODN, ODRORIR, and SON. To her dismay, Odin gulped down the entire contents of the vats, turned himself into an eagle, and flew off to Asgard. He was closely pursued by Suttung, who had tasted the mead and so knew some magic and could change his shape to that of a powerful eagle. But the gods had lit a great fire just outside the walls of Asgard. Suttung fell into this and was burned to death.

Odin spat the precious mead into the vessels that the gods eagerly held out, but in his haste to escape Suttung, he spilled some of the mead, which fell to Earth (MIDGARD). That is how some lucky humans acquired the gift of poetry.

**Mimir: How Odin Lost His Eye** Mimir was an ancient being noted for his wisdom. According to one myth, Mimir was the guardian of a sacred well (known as MIMIR'S WELL) that gave knowledge to those who drank from it. Odin so coveted wisdom that he gave up one of his eyes to Mimir to gain the privilege of drinking from the well. Mimir placed the eye in the well, where it shone as brilliantly as the Moon.

**Odin's Names** Odin had more than 150 names and attributes. Here are just a few of them:

Alfodr, All-Father, Father of the Gods
Baleyg, Flaming-Eyed
Bileyg, Shifty-Eyed
Fjolnir, Wide in Wisdom
GRIMNIR, Hooded One
Valfodr, Father of the Slain
Ygg, Awful

**ODRORIR** A cauldron. One of the three containers into which the DWARFS poured the MEAD of poetry (see under ODIN). The others were called BODN and SON.

**OLVALDI** JOTUN father of storm giants THIAZZI, IDI, and GANG. Olvaldi left such a large amount of gold to his sons that no scales could weigh it, so the sons measured it out in giant mouthfuls after their father's death.

See also "Skade and Niord," under SKADE.

**OTR** Son of HREIDMAR and brother of REGIN and FAFNIR. Otr was a SHAPE-SHIFTER and usually took the form of an otter. He was killed by the trickster god, LOKI. Hreidmar demanded as ransom enough gold to cover the dead otter's pelt and to fill its insides.

This myth is told by SNORRI STURLUSON in the *PROSE EDDA* and is mentioned in the *POETIC EDDA* and the late 13th-century *VOLSUNGA SAGA*.

In the *Reginsmal*, part of the *Poetic Edda*, the story of Otr also forms a preface to the SIGURD legends, in which Hreidmar is murdered by his sons REGIN and FAFNIR. Fafnir then steals the dwarf's treasure for himself and turns himself into a frightful dragon, the better to guard it. In the end, the hero Sigurd slays the dragon.

**Otr's Ransom** Something of a magician, Otr often took the form of an otter. One day ODIN, his brother HOENIR, and his blood brother LOKI were walking by a stream in MIDGARD. They saw an otter. Loki threw a stone at it and killed it. Then he picked up the otter and flung it over his shoulder.

The three came to the prosperous farmhouse of Hreidmar and asked for shelter for the night. At first Hreidmar was welcoming enough, but when he saw the otter, he shouted in rage and grief, for the dead creature was his son.

Hreidmar summoned his other two sons, Regin and Fafnir. Then, with his magic spells, he disarmed the gods and bound them. Now the gods recognized Hreidmar as the master magician of the trolls and DWARFS. He was very powerful indeed.

Odin told Hreidmar that he and his companions would pay whatever ransom he asked, for they had slain his son—but unknowingly, thinking that the creature was a real otter. Justice demanded that Hreidmar should be paid for his misfortune, but there was no need to start a blood feud.

Calmed by Odin's fairness, Hreidmar and his sons demanded that the otter's skin should be stuffed with gold inside and the outside covered with gold until not a whisker could be seen.

Odin and Hoenir agreed among themselves that, sly and cunning as he was, Loki would be the best one to go out and find enough gold for the awesome task, for the otter skin was growing bigger by the minute.

Freed of his bonds, Loki went straight to the place where he had killed the otter and stared down into the water. Soon he saw what he was looking for, an enormous pike guarding the entrance to an underwater cave that gleamed with gold. The pike was the dwarf ANDVARI, keeper of the fabled treasure.

Quickly Loki sped to the island of HLESEY where RAN, the ogress of the oceans, lived with her husband, AEGIR, god of the sea. Loki borrowed from her the cruel net with which she dragged drowning sailors to her underwater realm. With the net, Loki had no difficulty scooping up the pike. He landed it on the bank where it lay gasping and gradually changed into the ungainly shape of the dwarf.

To save his life, Andvari gave up his entire hoard of gold but for a single ring. This he begged Loki not to take from him.

Loki snatched up the ring and put it on his finger. Andvari laid a terrible curse upon the ring, vowing that anyone who wore it would be smitten with ill fortune and death.

The eyes of Hreidmar and his sons glittered greedily when they saw the gold. Odin, Hoenir, and Loki stuffed the otter's pelt and then made a blanket of gold all around the outside of it. Hreidmar examined it critically then pointed out a whisker that was exposed. Odin had seen Andvari's ring on Loki's finger. Loki pulled it off and laid it on the whisker.

Thus was Otr's ransom paid and the three travelers allowed to go, but not without a parting shot from Loki. He told Hreidmar that he and his sons were doomed to ill fortune and death, for that was the curse of Andvari.

**OTTAR** The human lover of the goddess FREYA. He built an altar to Freya and offered sacrifices. Freya helped him win a bet by turning him into her BOAR, HILDISVINI, and taking him to visit the giantess and seeress HYNDLA. Hyndla revealed that Ottar was the son of Instein and the priestess Hledis and that SIGURD, the greatest of Germanic heroes, was among his ancestors.

# P

**POETIC EDDA** A collection of poems on mythological and legendary themes, written down from the oral tradition by many different poets at different times between the eighth and 13th centuries. The *Poetic Edda* was called the *Elder Edda* because most of its material predates the 13th-century PROSE EDDA by SNORRI STURLUSON.

Among other manuscripts, the *Poetic Edda* consists of

- The CODEX REGIUS, which contains some 30 mythical and heroic poems, probably written about 1270 and discovered by Icelandic bishop Brynjólfur Sveinsson in 1643. It was erroneously called *Saemund's Edda* in old references, after the Icelandic bishop SAEMUND SIGFÚSSON, who was once thought to have written the poems.
- The *Arnamagnean Collection*, another, smaller group of poems that includes "Balder's Dreams" (see under BALDER).
- The VOLUSPA, an account of the origins of the world, its present state, its destruction at RAGNAROK, and the new world.

Poems of the *Poetic Edda* include

- *Alvismal (Lay of ALVIS)*
- *Flateyjarbok (Book of the Flat Island*, source of the myth about HYNDLA)
- GRIMNISMAL (*Lay of Grimnir*)
- *Harbarthsljoth (Lay of HARBARD)*
- HAVAMAL (*Words of the High One*)
- *Hymiskvitha (Lay of Hymir*, see under THOR)
- HYNDLULJOTH (*Lay of Hyndla*)
- LOKASENNA (*Loki's Mocking*)

- *Reginsmal (Lay of REGIN)*
- RIGSTHULA (*Lay of Rig*)
- SKIRNISMAL (*Lay of Skirnir*)
- SVIPDAGSMAL (*Lay of Svipdag*)
- THRYMSKVITHA (*Lay of Thrym*)
- VAFTHRUDNISMAL (*Lay of Vafthrudnir*)

Other poems in the *Poetic Edda* deal with mortal heroes (rather than gods) of the Northlands, for example SIGURD.

**PROSE EDDA** A manual for poets and scholars written circa 1220 by Icelandic poet, historian, and chieftain SNORRI STURLUSON (1179–1241). It is a handbook of Norse mythology, designed as a guide for poets to encourage them to write in the style of the ancient poets of the VIKING Age. Because it was written later than the POETIC EDDA (eighth–13th centuries), it was known as the *Younger Edda* and sometimes as the *Snorra Edda*.

The *Prose Edda* consists mostly of

- GYLFAGINNING (*The Deceiving of Gylfi*), which tells the myths of the Norse gods and GIANTS. It is an important source for some of the tales.
- SKALDSKAPARMAL (*Poetic Diction*), a listing of the condensed metaphors, called KENNINGS, frequently used in Viking poetry. Two examples of kennings are "Sif's hair" for "gold" (see TREASURES OF THE DWARFS), and "Kvasir's blood" for "poetry" (see "The Mead of Poetry," under ODIN). This work also contains some mythological and legendary tales.
- *Hattatal (The Meters of Poetry)* A poem by Snorri about King Haakon and Duke Skuli of NORWAY during the years 1221 and 1223.

For mythologists, the major interest of the *Prose Edda* is in *Gylfaginning*.

Snorri wrote this guide to old Icelandic poetry and mythology when Christianity was well established in Iceland and knowledge about the old gods and their adventures was dying out. He sought to preserve the ancient knowledge. Sometimes Snorri quotes from sources that are still available to modern scholars. At other times he quotes from poems and stories that are now lost.

# R

**RAGNAROK** (Doom of the Gods) The final battle between the gods, headed by ODIN and the EIN-HERJAR on the side of good, and LOKI and the HRIMTHURSSAR (frost GIANTS) on the side of evil. It took place on the plain called VIGRID. Nearly all the participants were slain. The Sun and Moon were swallowed by wolves, the stars vanished, the sacred tree YGGDRASIL trembled, the ocean boiled, and SURT set the world on fire so that everything was reduced to cinders. However, BALDER and HODUR rose up from the underworld; VALI, VIDAR, MODI, MAGNI, and some others survived to live in a regener-ated world. A HUMAN couple, LIF and LIFTHRASIR, also survived and repeopled Earth.

Ragnarok is dealt with in the Icelandic poem VOLUSPA (*Sibyl's Prophecy*) and in the *PROSE EDDA*.

**Ragnarok, the Day of Doom** Ragnarok was the end of the world, the twilight of the gods, the final battle between the forces of good (the gods) and the forces of evil (the giants and the monsters of the underworld). After the death of Balder, the gods ban-ished Loki, the evil one, to MIDGARD (Middle Earth), but it was too late. The god of light and innocence had been killed. The gods knew that the day of doom was at hand and that they and all their worlds would perish.

First came a wave of ghastly crimes and bloody wars in Midgard. Brothers fought against brothers; there was murder and looting and other evil deeds. Then came FIMBULVETR the worst of all winters. It brought bitter cold and driving snow, screeching winds and black darkness. The Fimbulvetr lasted three years. People shivered and starved and lost all hope and goodness.

From IRONWOOD came the ravenous wolves SKOLL and HATI. Skoll caught up with SOL's chariot and swallowed the Sun, spilling her blood on the Earth. Hati devoured the Moon. The stars fell out of the sky, and the darkness was complete.

Then the Earth began to tremble and quake, and the WOLF FENRIR broke from his bonds, ready to seek vengeance on the gods who had tricked him. Loki, too, broke free. GARM, HEL's hound, was set free. Evil and destruction were loose on the land.

EGGTHER, the watchman of the giants, struck a note on his harp. The red cock FJALAR (1) crowed to the giants, while GULLINKAMBI screeched to the gods in VALHALLA and a third rooster, rust red, awakened all the dead in NIFLHEIM.

HEIMDALL, the watchman of the gods, lifted his horn, GIALAR, and blew it. All the AESIR and the Einherjar sprang up and donned their armor, ready for the battle to end all battles. First Odin galloped off on SLEIPNIR to MIMIR'S WELL to seek his wisdom. The NORNS regarded him with veiled faces, their web of life rent into shreds. No one knew what Odin learned from MIMIR the Wise. He rejoined the waiting army with a grim, sad face and led them into battle, hold-ing aloft his magic spear, GUNGNIR.

The sea began to boil like a cauldron, and its waves crashed on the shore, for JORMUNGAND, the Midgard Serpent, had risen up from the deep and was lashing and writhing his way toward the land, spew-ing venom from his jaws.

The horrid ship NAGLFAR, made from dead men's fingernails, drifted loose, packed with giants and steered by HRYM. It headed toward the battlefield, which was called Vigrid. The crew and passengers of Loki's ship were all the pale dead from the underworld.

Hel, the goddess of death, left Niflheim to join the fray, followed by the hound Garm and the dragon NITHOG, who flew over the battlefield gathering corpses for his sustenance.

Loki led the terrible army of evil. As they crossed BIFROST, the RAINBOW BRIDGE, it trembled and broke beneath them, but not before they had reached Vigrid.

Odin, the mighty leader of the gods, attacked first. He joined battle with the monster-wolf, Fenrir, whose slavering jaws grew wider and wider, stretching from heaven to Earth, until they swallowed up Odin.

Nearby THOR, the god of thunder, wrestled with Jormungand. In the deathly struggle, Thor killed the serpent, but Thor, too, died a gasping death from the beast's fatal venom.

Loki and Heimdall, lifelong enemies, killed each other.

FREY, the god of fertility, grappled with the fire god, SURT, in a lengthy battle. Frey had given away his magic sword long ago for love of GERDA, and now, without it, he was killed by the fire demon.

TYR, who had only one hand, fought bravely against Garm, and the two killed each other.

All around the battle raged, and all were doomed to perish. But Vidar, a son of Odin, avenged his father. On his foot he wore a boot made from all the strips of leather snipped off and saved by good cobblers for just this purpose. Vidar crushed his magic boot onto the lower jaw of Fenrir, and, using all his strength, tore the wolf apart.

With Odin and most of the other gods, heroes, giants, and monsters dead, Surt (who some say was Loki in another shape) flung his brands of fire all over Earth so that there was a great and terrible conflagration. All NINE WORLDS went up in flames, and at last the Earth sank into the boiling sea.

The idea of Ragnarok is similar to Christian and Asian conceptions of Judgment Day or doomsday.

At Ragnarok, Thor attacks the Midgard Serpent with his hammer while Odin does battle with Fenrir, the wolf. *(Anthony Mercatante)*

However, the dramatic descriptions of darkness, earthquakes, flood, fire, and ashes undoubtedly came straight from the Icelandic poets' own experiences of volcanic eruptions in their native land.

**The Regeneration**   After the terrible destruction of Ragnarok, all was not lost after all, for there was a rebirth: Two HUMANS emerged, some of the gods survived, green plants grew, and a new world was born.

Before she was devoured by the wolf, Sol had given birth to a daughter, as brilliant and burning as she. As this new Sun appeared, darkness vanished, and a new day dawned in a world that gradually, magically, became green and pleasant, with fields of corn growing where no seeds had been planted.

From the remains of the sacred tree, Yggdrasil, stepped a human man, Lif, and a human woman, Lifthrasir. They had been nourished by dew and were unhurt by Surt's fire. They would repeople the Earth.

Vidar and Vali survived, as did Modi and Magni, Thor's sons, who inherited his hammer, MJOLLNIR. Balder came back from the dead, leading his blind brother, Hodur. HOENIR (VILI) appeared and so did LOTHUR (VE), Odin's brothers. They went to IDAVOLL, which had remained unscorched, and there they built new mansions, the greatest of which was GIMLÉ, roofed with gold. Another was Brimir, on the place called Okolnir (Never Cold). SINDRI rose up in the mountains of NIDAFJOLL. All these places were good. But there was also a hall on NASTROND, the shore of corpses. All its doors faced north to greet the shrieking winds. The walls were made of writhing snakes that poured their venom into a river that flowed through the hall. This was the new underworld, full of murderers and thieves, and when they died, NITHOG, who had survived, was there to feed upon the corpses.

The AESIR walked on the new green grass of Idavoll and talked about the past and their dear, perished friends. They played chess with the golden pieces that they found on the ground, and they thought with wonder about the new life of the Earth.

## RAINBOW BRIDGE   The common name for BIFROST, the bridge that stretched between the human world and the world of the gods, between Earth and heaven. This bridge was made by the gods in three colors—red, blue, and green—giving Bifrost its common nickname.

Only in the writings of 13th-century Icelandic historian SNORRI STURLUSON was the image of the rainbow associated with Bifrost, according to Old Norse experts. Earlier forms of this Norse myth refer to the Milky Way as the bridge that joins heaven and Earth.

**RAN** (Robber)   The wife of AEGIR, JOTUN lord of the sea. She lived with Aegir beneath the island of HLESEY, in coral caves. She dragged drowning sailors down to her realm in her fishing net, which either she or LOKI invented. Her halls were lighted only by the gleam of gold, reminiscent of the phosphorescent glow of the sea. It is said that she felt kindly toward dead sailors who had some gold in their possession to help her light her halls. In "Otr's Ransom," (under OTR), Loki borrows Ran's drowning net to catch the DWARF ANDVARI; in "The Pursuit of Loki-Salmon," Loki himself is trapped in a net.

**RATATOSK**   The squirrel who scampered up and down the World Tree, YGGDRASIL. He spread gossip and carried insults between NITHOG, the dragon who nibbled at the roots of the tree, and the EAGLE who sat in the topmost branches.

**RATI**   The name of the auger used by the giant BAUGI to drill a hole into the mountain HNITBORG (see "The Mead of Poetry," under ODIN).

**RAVEN**   A large, black bird, *Corvus corax*, a member of the crow family. The raven is commonly found in northern Europe, North America, and northern Asia. The raven was a symbol of ODIN, chief god among the AESIR gods. Odin kept two ravens, HUGIN (Thought) and MUNIN (Mind). Odin sent these ravens out into the world each daybreak, and they returned by breakfast time to tell Odin of what they had seen and learned. In an early NORSE poem, *HRAFNAGALDUR ODINS (Odin's Raven Chant)*, Odin sends the ravens to the underworld to investigate the disappearance of the goddess IDUNN.

The raven was a common symbol in many mythologies, sometimes as a sign of evil owing to its habits as a scavenger and sometimes as a sign of good. In Norse mythology, ravens played both roles. As representatives of Odin's mind and thoughts, ravens symbolized his power to see into the future. As symbols of the battlefield, they represented Odin's welcoming to his palace VALHALLA the spirits of slain HUMAN heroes who died in battle. Viking war flags carried symbols of ravens, as Odin's servants.

**REGIN**  Son of the magician HREIDMAR and brother of FAFNIR and OTR. After Fafnir killed Hreidmar and stole his treasure, Regin adopted the young hero, SIGURD, and ordered him to kill Fafnir, who had turned himself into a dragon. Regin was later killed by Sigurd.

**RIG**  The main character in *RIGSTHULA*, an ancient poem, part of the *POETIC EDDA*. The introduction to this poem in the surviving manuscripts says Rig is HEIMDALL, but modern scholars agree that an editor of the manuscript made that assumption and addition.

**Rig-Heimdall and the Races of Men**  Heimdall was the WATCHMAN OF THE GODS. He seldom left his post on BIFROST, the RAINBOW BRIDGE. But one day, at ODIN's suggestion, Heimdall went down to MIDGARD (Middle Earth) disguised as a mortal man. He left behind his horn, GIALAR, his sword, and his golden-topped steed, and took the name Rig.

Rig wandered along the seashore at the edge of the world. When evening came he saw a rickety old hut. Rig knocked and the door creaked open. It was dark and smoky inside, but Rig-Heimdall with his keen eyes could see Ai and Edda (Great-Grandfather and Great-Grandmother) and gave them his golden smile. They shared their miserable meal with him. Rig was so courteous and friendly that they shared their bed, too, allowing the sweet-talking god to sleep warmly between their two thin bodies. He shared their food and their bed for three days and three nights, then went on his way.

Nine months after the god's visit Edda gave birth to a son. His parents named him Thrall. The boy was sturdy and strong and grew to be very good at all the hard and heavy chores that laborers must do: chopping wood, digging the earth, building huts, tending the pigs and GOATS, gathering food, burning peat. When Thrall grew up he married Esne, another hard worker, and their children and their children's children were the peasants and laborers of the world.

The evening after leaving Ai and Edda, Rig came to a big farm where he found Afi and Amma (Grandfather and Grandmother). Afi's beard was neatly trimmed and Amma's hair was smooth and silvery. They both wore clean and simple clothes. Rig gave them his golden smile. They shared their nourishing meal with him. Rig was so courteous and friendly that they shared their bed, too, allowing the sweet-talking god to sleep warmly between their sturdy bodies. He shared their food and their bed for three days and three nights, then went on his way.

Nine months after the god's visit, Amma gave birth to a son. The parents named him Freeman. The boy was healthy and ruddy, and he grew to be very good at all the work that a proud farmer must do: building fine houses and sturdy barns and learning the skills of the blacksmith, the reaper of corn, and the tender of fine animals. When Freeman grew up he married a strapping girl named Hussif. She knew how to spin and weave; she sewed a fine seam and baked good bread. Their children and their children's children became the farmers, landholders, and craftsmen of the world.

The evening after leaving Afi and Amma, Rig came to a great mansion where he found Father Squire and Mother Lady. Their clothes were rich and glittering with jewels. Rig gave them his golden smile, and the handsome couple invited him to dinner. A long table was covered with a linen cloth and set with silver wine jugs and goblets and pewter platters. The servants brought in mounds of delicious meats and fruits. Rig was so courteous and friendly that Lady and Squire shared their luxurious bed with him, allowing the sweet-talking god to sleep warmly between their two shapely bodies. Rig shared their food and their bed for three days and three nights, then went on his way.

Nine months after the god's visit, Lady gave birth to a son. The parents named him Earl. The boy was tall and handsome, with golden hair and a golden smile, and he grew to be a fine horseman, skilled with both spear and sword as well as with a bow and arrow. When Earl grew up he married a rich and graceful girl named Princess. Her skin was soft and her fingers long. She played beautifully on the lute and her voice was the envy of the nightingale. She made Earl very rich and happy. Their children and their children's children became the kings and queens of many lands of the world.

Rig-Heimdall transported himself to the time when Earl was still a young lad. The god appeared before Earl in a forest grove, bringing with him some sticks with strangely carved markings on them. Rig taught Earl, his son, the secrets of the RUNES and much wisdom about the good and evil in the world so that Earl and his children and grandchildren could become fine and just rulers of their kingdoms.

**RIGSTHULA** An ancient poem found in the POETIC EDDA that tells the story of the beginnings of humankind and of the classes within society.

The importance of this poem in understanding Norse mythology is heavily debated among scholars and experts. The introduction to the 14th-century manuscript in which this poem was found says that RIG, the main character, is actually the god HEIMDALL, who watched over the land of the gods; however, nowhere in the poem itself is Rig identified with Heimdall, and many scholars question why others say Rig is Heimdall. Modern experts also suggest that the poem is older than its introduction and that the editor of the manuscript chose to give Heimdall credit for being Rig. In the manuscript in which it was found, the end of the *Rigsthula* is missing.

Experts are unsure of the age of the poem. Some say it was written as early as the ninth century A.D., others as late as the 13th century.

**RINDA** (RIND) Daughter of BILLING, king of the Ruthenians; mate of the god ODIN; mother of VALI (2). She appears only once in the existing Norse manuscripts, as the temporary wife of Odin. Rinda is a personification of the hard frozen rind of the Earth. At first, she resists the wooing of Odin (the Sun) but finally succumbs to his warmth and gives birth to Vali, the light god of spring.

**ROSKVA** The farmer EGIL's daughter who becomes the god THOR's servant, along with her brother THIALFI. Thor took the brother and sister to be his eternal servants after Thialfi had disobeyed his command not to mutilate the bones of his goats.

**ROSTIOFF** In some tellings of the myths Rostioff is the wizard who prophesied that from the union of ODIN and RINDA a son, VALI (2), would be born and that Vali would avenge the death of BALDER. The wizard lived in Lapland.

**ROWAN** A mountain ash tree of the rose family, not related to the common ASH tree. A sturdy tree, it has dense white blossoms and clusters of red fruit well loved by birds. Old superstitions say that the tree has protective qualities, especially against witches. (It is sometimes called witch wood or witchen tree). In Scotland to this day, it is often planted near the front door of a house. In Norse mythology it is called "Thor's Salvation" or "Thor's Tree of Deliverance" because it saved THOR from drowning in the VIMUR River.

**RUNES** (That Which Is Secret) Ancient letters or symbols used in the earliest alphabets of the German tribes of northern Europe, including the NORSE, from the second to the 12th centuries. Runic inscriptions occur most commonly in SCANDINAVIA and

Examples of runic alphabets *(New York Public Library Picture Collection)*

parts of the British Isles. The characters consisted of perpendicular, slanting, and curved lines, well adapted to being carved on wood, stone, and metal. Magical and mysterious powers were associated with runes.

According to Norse mythology, knowledge of runes was introduced by the god ODIN, who hanged himself from the branches of the sacred tree, YGGDRASIL, for nine days and nine nights until fallen twigs from the tree spelled out the secrets of the runes.

After the establishment of Christianity in the north, runes were looked down upon as pagan. Nonetheless, in Scandinavia their use continued after the Middle Ages in manuscripts as well as in inscriptions on stone, metal, and wood.

# S

**SAEHRIMNIR** (Sooty) The magic BOAR that each day was killed and cooked by ANDHRIMNIR (Sooty Faced) in the giant cauldron ELDHRIMNIR (Soot Blackened), and eaten by the gods and heroes at VALHALLA.

**SAEMING** A son of the great Norse god ODIN, perhaps invented by the 13th-century Icelandic historian SNORRI STURLUSON or by rulers of ancient NORWAY.

According to Snorri in the introduction to three of his great works, Odin was a powerful leader from central Asia who traveled north through Europe to SWEDEN, establishing two of his sons as rulers of kingdoms along the way. Near the end of his journey, Odin traveled north to the coast. There he made his son Saeming king. This interpretation of myths as the stories of real HUMANS is known as euhemerism.

Many historical rulers of Norway traced their ancestry to Saeming, and he became a father figure, a great ancestor, to the powerful families in that region. Scholars believe the rulers of the lands in SCANDINAVIA may have created the stories of Saeming and his brothers to connect their histories to the legends of the gods.

In another part of his *PROSE EDDA*, Snorri also wrote that SKADE, daughter of the frost giant THIAZZI, was Saeming's mother.

**SAEMUND SIGFÚSSON** (Saemund the Wise, Saemund the Learned) (1056–1133) Icelandic historian and Catholic priest; author of an important history of the kings of Norway that has been lost. Later authors made use of Saemund's history and discussed its importance in their own works.

Before 1900, literary scholars and experts believed Saemund wrote the *POETIC EDDA*, a collection of ancient Norse poetry found in the *CODEX REGIUS*. They referred to these poems as *Saemund's Edda*. Based on detailed studies of the language and style of these old poems, experts no longer believe that Saemund had any connection to the *Poetic Edda*.

**SAGA (1)** An Old NORSE word meaning "story." The sagas were stories in prose or verse dating from the early 11th to the mid-14th centuries, first written down about 1200. There were family sagas about early Icelandic settlers; sagas of the kings, which were semihistorical stories about the kings of Norway; and heroic sagas, which told of legendary heroes and fantastic adventures. The *VOLSUNGA SAGA* (late 13th century) is a good example of a heroic saga.

**SAGA (2)** A female goddess, one of the ASYNJUR. (The first *a* in her name is a long *a*, making the pronunciation different from SAGA [1], a type of story.) Little is known of Saga except that she lived in the great hall known as Sokkvabekk, where she often spent the day drinking from golden goblets with ODIN. Some scholars suggest that Saga was another name for FRIGG, Odin's wife, for Saga means "she who knows all things" and this was a trait Frigg shared with her husband.

**SAXO GRAMMATICUS** Danish scholar of the 13th century who wrote *GESTA DANORUM*, a multivolume, partly mythical history of the Danes. In it Saxo recounts many myths of DENMARK (including that of Hamlet) and NORWAY. Saxo's approach to the myths and the people in them was rather harsh and unsympathetic compared to that of the Icelandic writer SNORRI STURLUSON.

**SCANDINAVIA** A region in northwestern Europe. NORWAY and SWEDEN form the great peninsula once known as Scandia and now known as the Scandinavian peninsula. DENMARK's Jutland peninsula and the islands the lie between it and the Scandinavian peninsula, as well as the Faeroe Islands and ICELAND, which lie in the Atlantic Ocean to the west and northwest of Norway, are often considered part of the region.

The people of Scandinavia share similar languages, histories, and cultures. Norwegian, Swedish, Danish, and Icelandic all share roots with the Germanic languages. Their ancestors spoke Old NORSE, a name that has often been used to refer to the people of Scandinavia as well as the ancient language. In 400 B.C., the Germanic peoples of north central Europe began moving northward and building settlements in Scandinavia, living next to or pushing aside the native people of those lands. By A.D. 600, nation-states had begun to take shape in these regions, and language changes separated these immigrant peoples from the cultures of their origins. Around this time the VIKINGS, a powerful people, began centuries of conquest across northern Europe, including England, Finland, and parts of eastern Russia.

Much of the information of the mythology of the Norse has survived in the records and manuscripts of the Scandinavian nations and on the intricate and complex stone carvings found throughout the region. Scholars have pieced together the stories of the gods, goddesses, enemies, and kingdoms of this mythology from scattered sources. From Iceland to the west and Finland to the east, the Arctic Circle to the north and the bogs of low-lying Denmark to the south, archaeologists have for almost two centuries uncovered the story of Scandinavia's past, including the spectacular finds of SHIPS AND SHIP BURIALS near Oseberg, Norway, in 1904 and at Sutton Hoo in East Anglia, England, first excavated in 1939.

**SEID** A special form of magic or witchcraft, often socially objectionable, containing highly ritualistic ceremonies and oaths. In powerful cultic ceremonies, priestesses summoned this magic so they could see into the future; arrange bad luck, illness, or death for an enemy; or transfer the mind and strength of one person into another. Often leaders would seek out the help of people with these magical powers in times of crisis.

Women were the primary practitioners of seid, which reportedly had a strong sexual impact on the magicians. In the ceremonies, the priestess wore a special costume made of fur and featuring a prominent headdress.

According to Norse mythology, FREYA, a VANIR goddess, shared the gift of seid with the great AESIR god ODIN and the other gods and goddesses. Odin became the chief practitioner of this magic among all of the Aesir gods. Freya is said to have never used her powers.

**SERPENT** Word often used in mythology, religion, and folklore to denote nonspecific reptiles, such as snakes and dragons and also sea monsters. In Norse mythology, the DRAGON NITHOG chewed at the roots of the sacred tree, YGGDRASIL, and JORMUNGAND, the Midgard Serpent, encircled the Earth with his tail in his mouth and spewed poisonous fumes at RAGNAROK. The great god, ODIN, turned himself into a serpent to enter the cave where he found the MEAD of poetry. FAFNIR turned himself into a dragon to guard his treasure (see "Otr's Ransom," under OTR). The gods placed a serpent over LOKI's head after they had bound him to a rock.

**SESSRUMNIR** (Rich in Seats) The hall of the goddess FREYA where she welcomed the spirits of slain warriors and heroes, whom she shared with the war god, ODIN. Sessrumnir was located in the part of ASGARD known as FOLKVANGER, the realm of Freya. It is said to have had as much room for its guests as did VALHALLA, the palace where Odin welcomed his share of fallen warriors.

**SHAPE-SHIFTER** (Shape Changer) Gods and GIANTs magically change form often within the stories of Norse mythology. This was a complete physical transformation, not merely a surface disguise. Most commonly they took the shape of EAGLEs or FALCONs to fly swiftly over land.

The supreme god ODIN had the power to change shape at will and took on many different identities to walk among humans. He and FREYA preferred the form of the hawk for their supernatural travels. LOKI, though, was the most famous shape changer, for he would change gender as well as form. In the story of the GIANT MASTER BUILDER, Loki became a mare to lure away the giant's stallion. In the story of the making of the *TREASURES OF THE DWARFS*, he became a fly to pester the dwarfs.

Giants, too, changed shape. One became an eagle to steal the gods' dinner. Another took the shape of a man to trick the gods.

**SHIPS AND SHIP BURIALS** Ships were an important part of NORSE culture. The Norse depended on ships not only for fishing and trading but for expanding their empires. The VIKING seafarers roamed from their northern strongholds as far south as the Iberian Peninsula (modern Spain and Portugal), Italy, and Sicily and as far east as Russia, Constantinople, and Baghdad. A Viking navigator, Leif Eriksson, sailed to North America in about the year 1000, almost five centuries before Christopher Columbus set foot in the Americas. The Vikings also colonized ICELAND and Greenland.

Viking ships were longships, with graceful, upward-curving bows and sterns, often carved with elaborate designs. They were powered by oarsmen and sails.

Ships were so venerated that when a distinguished person died, he was put aboard his ship, which was then set afire and sent out to sea. In the myth of BALDER, the god was set aboard his ship, HRINGHORNI, along with his dead wife, his horse, and some of his treasures. *Hringhorni* was then set afire and sent out to sea.

In recent years archaeological digs have uncovered various burial ships in SCANDINAVIA and England. Along with the bones of dead people and

This graceful vessel, found at the Gokstad, Norway, burial site, probably belonged to a ninth-century Viking chieftain. *(©University Museum of Cultural Heritage—University of Oslo, Norway; photographed by Mittet)*

animals, they contained ancient weapons, chariots, jewelry, ornaments, food, and utensils—all the necessities for the comfort of the dead in the afterlife. In Sutton Hoo, in East Anglia, England, the remains of an 80-foot ship were uncovered along with treasures but no bones of the dead. It is thought that the hero may have disappeared at sea, or perhaps he had been given a Christian burial while his treasures were buried according to a more ancient pagan custom. The Sutton Hoo ship dates from the seventh century. Other graves found in East Anglia were the tombs of humble people, including children who were buried with toylike ships. In early English literature the account in *Beowulf* (recorded about A.D. 1000) describes the voyage of Skyld, first king of the Danes, on his funeral ship.

The ship was so important in Norse culture that it was carried as a symbol in processions long after Christianity had become established. Medieval craftsmen built mock ships (symbols of life and of death and of the journey in between) to be carried in religious processions. So beautiful and elaborate were these ships that eventually they were made collapsible to be folded up and stored inside the church until the next procession. It is thought that this medieval practice may have influenced the description of SKID-BLADNIR, the marvelous ship made for the god FREY. *Skinbladnir* could be shrunk and folded to fit inside a pouch when not in use.

## SIEGFRIED   See SIGURD.

**SIF**   THOR's golden-haired wife, goddess of grain and of fertility. She was the mother of ULL, Thor's stepson. The mischiefmaker LOKI cut off Sif's hair while she slept. He was forced to replace it with strands of gold crafted by the DWARFS (see *TREASURES OF THE DWARFS*).

**SIGURD** (Siegfried, in German)   A human hero of Germanic legend, possibly of historical origin. He is the chief character in the 13th-century *VOLSUNGA SAGA* and in *Reginsmal* (see POETIC EDDA). The Sigurd stories are prefaced by the Norse myth "Otr's Ransom" (see under OTR), though it is believed that originally there was no connection between the two.

**SIGYN** (SIGUNN, SIGRYN, SIGUNA; Victory Giver)   The wife of the trickster god, LOKI, and the mother of NARFI and VALI (1).

When the gods finally trapped Loki and bound him, placing a SERPENT over his head, Sigyn stayed by her husband's side. In a bowl she caught the venom that dripped from the serpent's jaws. When she turned aside to empty the bowl, some venom fell on Loki, and he writhed with pain, causing earthquakes on MIDGARD. Sigyn stayed with Loki until RAGNAROK, the end of the world.

In this 12th-century carving from Hylestad, Norway, Regin, the smith, repairs Sigurd's sword. *(New York Public Library Picture Collection)*

Loyal Sigyn, Loki's wife, catches venom from the serpent that hangs over Loki's head. *(Anthony Mercatante)*

**SIMUL** The pole on which BIL AND YUKI carried their pail of water (see "Sun and Moon," under CREATION).

**SINDRI** (Sparky, Slag) The name of the magnificent golden hall that will stand shining upon a mountain after RAGNAROK, the final battle between the gods and the GIANTS at the end of time. Sindri also refers to the good and righteous people who will dwell within this splendid palace.

**SINGASTEIN** The place where LOKI and HEIMDALL, transformed into seals, fought over FREYA's necklace, which Loki had stolen.

**SJOFN** A female goddess named by 13th-century Icelandic historian SNORRI STURLUSON in his prose work GYLFAGINNING. Very little is known of Sjofn except that, according to Snorri, she had the job of influencing people to fall in love with each other.

**SKADE** (SKADI; Destruction) Daughter of the HRIMTHURSSAR (frost giant) THIAZZI and wife of NIORD, the VANIR god of the seas and of sailors and fishermen. Skade was the goddess of winter, skiers, and hunters. After her father's death she went to ASGARD, the home of the gods, to choose a husband from among them. She and Niord found that they could not live happily together, for Skade did not like Niord's seashore home, NOATUN, and Niord did not like the bleak cold of THRYMHEIM, Skade's home.

In the story "Loki's Punishment" (see under LOKI), Skade placed a venomous serpent over the head of the trickster god. She is the personification of the cold-hearted northern winter that can be touched only briefly by the warmth of the summer sun (Niord) and the cheerful hearth fire (Loki).

**Skade and Niord** In SNORRI STURLUSON's *PROSE EDDA*, the story of the marriage between Skade, goddess of winter, and Niord, the god associated with the seas and seafarers, immediately follows "Idunn's Apples" (see under IDUNN), in which Thiazzi, Skade's father, is killed by the gods after stealing the apples. At the news of his death, Skade was full of rage. She put on her shining armor and her weapons and strode across BIFROST to ASGARD, the home of the AESIR.

The gods were at peace, glad to feel young again now that Idunn was back with her magic apples of youth. They asked Skade if she would take gold in payment for her father's death, for such was the custom of the Norse.

Skade scornfully replied that she had all the gold she needed. When OLVALDI had died, he had left much gold to his sons, Thiazzi, GANG, and IDI, and now she had all of Thiazzi's share. Instead, she demanded a husband from among the gods.

The gods conferred and agreed it would be wise to let the icy giantess have her way. There was one condition: Skade must choose her husband by the look of his feet, not by his face.

Skade agreed, but she, too, had a condition. The gods must make her laugh, for she was full of rage and her heart was cold.

The strange bargain was struck, and the gods stood barefoot behind a curtain that hid all but their feet. One pair of feet at once struck Skade as more

Skade chose her husband by pointing to the feet that she liked best. *(Anthony Mercatante)*

beautiful than the rest. They must belong to the beautiful god BALDER, she thought. She announced her choice.

Out stepped NIORD, the VANIR god, lord of the seas and of seafarers, and the father of FREY and FREYA. Skade was disappointed. Bitterly, she asked the gods to make her laugh.

LOKI, the trickster god who had been partially responsible for Thiazzi's death, had set his quick mind to work as soon as he had heard Skade's requests. Now he led forward one of THOR's rambunctious billy GOATS, and the two played such lively and hilarious antics that Skade and all the gods laughed until their sides ached.

As a wedding present for Skade, ODIN took Thiazzi's eyes from his pouch and hurled them into the heavens, where they shone brightly as twin stars.

Niord took his new wife to his home, NOATUN, by the seashore. Skade did not like the sunshine, the sea, the sound of the waves, or the cry of the gulls. Niord then went with Skade to Thrymheim, her sunless, freezing mountain home, but Niord did not like the howling of the wolves, the wind, the bare mountains, or the terrible cold.

The two tried to divide their time between the two homes: nine days in Niord's Noatun and nine in Skade's Thrymheim. But Skade spent more and more time in the cold mountains, a dark shape speeding over the snow in her snowshoes, bringing death to wolves and bears from her quiver full of arrows. She is the goddess of skiers and hunters. ULL, son of SIF and stepson of Thor, is also the god of winter and of skiers and hunters, but, as far as we know, Skade and Ull were not related.

**SKALD** (SCALD) In Old NORSE, a poet. In the study of Norse mythology, the term refers to a specialist among poets who served in the courts of kings, powerful rulers, and chieftains. These poets often wrote about the great deeds of their leaders and of the gifts the leaders gave them. Skalds used complex, elaborate patterns and KENNINGs to create a distinct form known today as SKALDIC POETRY.

The oldest of the known skalds, Bragi Boddason inn gamli (Bragi Boddason the Old), lived in the ninth century A.D. Scholars believe he was the court poet of the Swedish king Björn. His poem *Ragnarsdrapa* describes scenes from mythology as portrayed on a shield, including THOR fishing for JORMUNGAND, the Midgard Serpent; GEFION plowing away part of SWEDEN; and the story of Hild encouraging her father Hogni and Hedin, her abductor, to fight, as told in the *HJADNINGAVIG*.

**SKALDIC POETRY** A complex form of NORSE poetry that relies on precise numbers and stresses of syllables in each half-line of the poem. Skaldic poetry mainly consists of KENNINGs, or poetic, often mythical, metaphors, to present meaning to the audience. Much information about Norse mythology is preserved in this form of poetry.

Skaldic poems are distinct from the works in the POETIC EDDA in several important ways. Most skaldic poems are the works of named SKALDs, or specialist poets. Eddic poems, on the other hand, are anonymous and timeless. Skaldic poets counted syllables carefully, while eddic poets wrote in a freer verse. Skaldic poets used myth to praise real heroes, and eddic poems are about the myths themselves.

Existing skaldic poetry is preserved in ancient manuscripts written centuries after the lives of the poets, who were part of a preliterate oral tradition. Some poems have survived in full, but of others only a stanza has survived.

**SKALDSKAPARMAL** (*Poetic Diction*)   A section in the *PROSE EDDA*; the source of the story "The Mead of Poetry" (see under ODIN).

**SKIDBLADNIR** (Wooden-Bladed)   The magic ship made by the DWARFS sons of IVALDI, and brought to FREY by LOKI (see *TREASURES OF THE DWARFS*). The ship was big enough to hold all the gods and their horses and equipment, yet small enough to be folded up and put away in a pouch when not in use. It could sail over land or through the air, as well as on the sea, and has been compared to a swift-moving cloud or a magic carpet.

See also SHIPS AND SHIP BURIALS.

**SKINFAXI**   The name of DAG's horse. Considered to be the best of horses, Skinfaxi pulled the day, that is, the Sun, through the sky. His gleaming mane lit up the heavens and the Earth.

**SKIRNIR** (Shining)   The servant of the shining god, FREY. He borrowed Frey's horse and sword and went on a long journey to woo the JOTUN maid GERDA for his lovesick master. In another myth, Skirnir was sent by the gods to ask the DWARFS to make them a magic chain with which to bind the wolf, FENRIR.

**SKIRNIR'S JOURNEY**   Poem in the *Codex Regius*, which forms part of the *POETIC EDDA*. Called "For Skirnis" in Icelandic, the poem tells of SKIRNIR's wooing of GERDA for his master, FREY.

**SKIRNISMAL** (*Lay of Skirnis*)   Poem in the *Arnamagnean Codex*, which forms part of the *POETIC EDDA*. Like *SKIRNIR'S JOURNEY*, it tells the story of SKIRNIR's

trip to woo the JOTUN maid GERDA for his master, FREY. In the *Arnamagnean Codex* the story is incomplete.

**SKOLL**   The terrible WOLF born in IRONWOOD, who pursues the chariot of the Sun and in the end, at RAGNAROK, devours it (see "Sun and Moon," under CREATION).

See also HATI and MANAGARM.

**SKRYMIR** (Big Fellow)   A very large giant encountered by THOR and LOKI and their servants on their way to UTGARD. Skrymir, sometimes called Vasty in English retellings, was most likely UTGARD-LOKI in disguise. He was so huge that Thor and his companions mistook his mitten for a large cabin, where they spent the night.

The giant Skrymir (Utgard-Loki) towers over the God Thor. (*Anthony Mercatante*)

**SKULD** (Future) One of the three NORNS, or Fates. She is pictured wearing a veil and carrying a scroll in her hands.

**SKY** In the Norse CREATION myth, the sky was made from the dome of the giant YMIR's skull. It was held up at the corners by four DWARFS, NORDI, SUDRI, AUSTRI, and VESTRI. It was lit by the SUN and the Moon (see "Sun and Moon," under CREATION); the stars were created from sparks borrowed from MUSPELLHEIM, the land of fire; and it was shaded by clouds made from Ymir's brains.

**SLEIPNIR** (Glider) ODIN's eight-legged horse, the offspring of SVADILFARI and LOKI, the SHAPESHIFTER god who disguised himself as a mare to tempt Svadilfari away from his work for GIANT MASTER BUILDER (see "Asgard's Wall and the Giant Master Builder," under ASGARD).

Sleipnir was no ordinary horse. He could gallop over the sea and through the air as well as on land and could outrun any horse in all the NINE WORLDS, including GULLFAXI. Sleipnir was able to journey to the world of the dead; he carried both HERMOD and ODIN there. At RAGNAROK, the end of the world, Sleipnir carried Odin into battle and was presumably killed by FENRIR, the WOLF, along with his master.

**SNORRI STURLUSON** (1179–1241) A leading figure in Norse literature, Snorri Sturluson was ICELAND's most distinguished author. He was the author of the PROSE EDDA, of *Heimskringla* (a history of Norwegian kings), and of *Hattatal* (a poem in praise of King Haakon and Duke Skuli of NORWAY), plus various sagas. One of Iceland's greatest chieftains, Snorri came from the powerful Sturlung dynasty. He was educated at Iceland's foremost cultural center, Oddi, where he received strong training in law, history, poetry, and the telling of sagas. He became renowned as a lawyer and a SKALD, or poet. Politically ambitious, Snorri was welcomed at all the Scandinavian courts. He acquired great wealth and power but was involved in numerous disputes and battles. He was finally slain in a political coup at the command of the king of Norway.

It would be difficult to exaggerate the importance of the *Prose Edda*, sometimes called the *Younger Edda* or the *Snorra Edda*. It gives the only complete picture of Norse mythology dating from the Middle Ages. The *Prose Edda* had great influence on medieval Icelandic literature and helped to preserve the ancient skaldic tradition.

**SNOTRA** (Clever) One of the minor goddesses named by SNORRI STURLUSON, who described her as clever and well behaved. Scholars suspect that she might have been created by Snorri.

**SOEG** The pail in which BIL AND YUKI carry water (see "Sun and Moon," under CREATION).

**SOL** (Sun) According to 13th-century Icelandic poet SNORRI STURLUSON, a servant of the SUN. Sol was the daughter of the human MUNDILFARI and the sister of MANI. The gods stole Sol and Mani from their father when they were children—or perhaps young adults, since Snorri says Sol was married to a man named Glen. The gods were offended that a HUMAN, Mundilfari, had named his children after the Sun and the Moon.

In Snorri's telling of their story, the gods put Sol to work in the heavens where she drove the chariot that carried the Sun through the sky. Two horses, ARVAKR and ALSVID, pulled the chariot. To protect the horses and Sol from the flaming heat of the Sun, which would burn up anything that came too close to it, the gods placed the shield SVALIN between them and the Sun.

The huge, evil WOLF SKOLL chased Sol and the Sun's chariot through the sky until RAGNAROK, when he caught and devoured the Sun.

Sol is rarely given human characteristics in Norse poetry. Only Snorri tells the story of her work in the heavens. An older poem, part of the POETIC EDDA, identifies Sol as the Sun, not a servant, and only names her and the Moon as children of Mundilfari. The Sun played only a small role in Norse mythology.

**SOLSTICE** The times of the year when the Sun reaches its extreme northern or southern points in its journey across the heavens. In the Northern Hemisphere the summer solstice is around June 21, and the winter solstice is around December 22. The word *solstice* is made up of two Latin words, *sol,* meaning "sun," and *sistit,* meaning "stands," because the Sun appears to stand still before it turns back on its apparent course. The longest day occurs at summer solstice and the shortest day at winter solstice. Both these days are times of rejoicing, especially in NORSE countries. MIDSUMMER EVE, on June 21, was Balder's Day, celebrated with bonfires and the observance of sunrise and sunset. Yuletide occurred at the time of the winter solstice, when people celebrated the beginning of the end of the winter months.

**SON** A jar. One of the three containers into which the DWARFS poured the MEAD of poetry (see "The Mead of Poetry," under ODIN). The other containers were called BODN and ODRORIR.

**STARKAD** A famous Norse hero who was both blessed and cursed by the gods. Starkad was the name of the main character of many heroic legends, and scholars suggest there may have been several different heroes with the same name. In the stories that survive there are two Starkads. One was the descendent of GIANTS who himself had six or eight arms. This Starkad, who had the last name Aludreng, was the grandfather of the most famous Starkad, the foster son of the god ODIN.

Odin remained in disguise as he helped raise the younger Starkad. Once Starkad witnessed a gathering of the gods, 12 of them sitting in chairs with an empty chair in the gathering. Only when Odin joined the gathering and sat in the empty chair did Starkad recognize his foster father for the god he was.

The mighty thunder god, THOR, hated Starkad. On one occasion, Odin wanted to honor the bravery of the warrior Starkad, but Thor wanted to harm the hero he so hated. Odin bestowed many blessings upon Starkad, among them success in battle, invincibility, great wealth, and great skill as a poet. Thor countered each positive gift with a negative consequence, causing Starkad to be seriously hurt in every battle, never enjoy his wealth, and never have anyone know of his poetry.

As a result of the conflicting favor and disfavor bestowed on him by the two gods, Starkad lived to be very old, but he committed notorious deeds, including killing the king whom he had earlier served with much honor.

Many sagas from ICELAND tell of the adventures of Starkad. In them, he is portrayed as old, misshapen, and gray haired.

**STARS** After they had created the Earth and the sky, ODIN and his brothers caught glowing embers and sparks from MUSPELLHEIM and threw them up into the SKY to be stars (see "The Sky," under CREATION). As time went on, they created new stars.

See also THIAZZI.

**SUDRI** (South) One of the four DWARFS named after the four cardinal compass directions. The others are AUSTRI (East), VESTRI (West), and NORDI (North). These four dwarfs are mentioned in early NORSE poetry, but only SNORRI STURLUSON gave Sudri and his companions the job of holding up the four corners of the sky.

**SUN** The Sun is mentioned frequently in Norse mythology, but only in one poem in the *POETIC EDDA* and in SNORRI STURLUSON's *PROSE EDDA* is it given the names SOL. Only Snorri tells the story of Sol's life, and in that story, she is a servant of the Sun.

The Sun disk, however, was a popular image in rock carvings and on brooches and ornaments from the Norse age. The disk was also carved into memorial stones. The Sun is also often represented as a wheel, both in objects made during the Norse age and in the surviving poetry from that time. The Sun is referred to as the "wheel of heaven."

FREY appears to be the god most closely connected to the Sun. Scholars often see his courtship of and marriage to the giantess GERDA as a legend of the Sun pursuing the frozen Earth (see CREATION).

**SUN AND MOON** The children of MUNDILFARI, who named his daughter SOL, which means "sun," and his son MANI, which means "moon." Older NORSE poems identify Mundilfari as the father of these children but do not discuss where he lived or what type of being he was. The 13th-century Icelandic poet SNORRI STURLUSON in his *PROSE EDDA* described Mundilfari as a HUMAN father. According to Snorri, the gods grew angry with this presumptuous human, stealing his children and putting them to work in the sky.

**SURT** (Black) The fire god with the flaming sword who set fire to the world at RAGNAROK. He is called the leader of the sons of MUSPELLHEIM, land of fire. Surt and the god FREY fought a long battle at Ragnarok, and Surt killed Frey.

**SURTSEY** An island south of and belonging to ICELAND, named for the Norse fire god, SURT. It was formed by a volcanic eruption from an underwater volcano, Sutur. The eruption began in 1963 and ended in 1967. Surtsey, the newest island on Earth, is now a nature reserve.

**SUTTUNG** (Heavy with Broth) A giant. Suttung was the son of GILLING, who was murdered by the DWARFS FJALAR (2) and GALAR, and the brother of BAUGI. His daughter was GUNLOD, the guardian of the MEAD of poetry (see under ODIN). Suttung hid the three containers of the MEAD in an underground cave of the mountain HNITBORG, where he and Gunlod lived. He would share it with no one. Odin, using his magic, succeeded in getting into the cave and stealing away the mead. Suttung was able to change himself into an EAGLE to chase Odin (who was also in eagle form), but Suttung fell into a fire that the gods had made at the walls of ASGARD, their home, and perished.

**SVADILFARI** The stallion belonging to the GIANT MASTER BUILDER who built the ASGARD wall. Svadilfari was a mighty animal, immensely powerful. He was lured from his task of helping the builder by a pretty mare (LOKI in disguise) and became the sire of SLEIPNIR, ODIN's eight-legged horse.

**SVALIN** (Iron Cool) The shield placed in SOL's chariot to protect her from the flames of the Sun (see "Sun and Moon," under CREATION).

**SVARTALFHEIM** (DARKALFHEIM) The realm of the black, or dark, elves, who were also called DWARFS. It lay deep underground, beneath the roots of the World Tree, YGGDRASIL. It was there that LOKI

went to ask the dwarfs, who were skilled craftsmen, to produce treasures for the gods (see TREASURES OF THE DWARFS).

**SVIPDAG** (Swift Day) The human son of the seeress GROA and the hero of SVIPDAGSMAL (Ballad of Svipdag) in the POETIC EDDA. Svipdag goes to NIFLHEIM to seek the advice of Groa. He summoned her from the grave to ask her the best way to woo and win MENGLOD, the fair maiden he loves. Groa chants him a series of charms that will protect him in his travels. Svipdag sets off to seek Menglod. In JOTUNHEIM he finds a massive gate guarded by the giant FJOLSVID. After a series of questions and answers in which Svipdag learns about the gods and giants and their worlds, the giant finally lets Svipdag enter the gates, where he finds the beautiful Menglod waiting for him with open arms.

**SVIPDAGSMAL** (Ballad of Svipdag) A poem found in the POETIC EDDA. It tells the story of SVIPDAG, the human son of the witch GROA, who seeks help from his dead mother to win the love of the beautiful giantess MENGLOD. Modern experts believe that the existing manuscript combines two older poems, Grogald and Fjolsvinnsmal, into one story.

**SWEDEN** A nation in northern Europe forming the eastern half of the Scandinavian peninsula. Sweden is part of SCANDINAVIA, which includes NORWAY, making up the western part of the peninsula, DENMARK, ICELAND, and the Faeroe Islands. Together these nations form the home of the NORSE culture and its mythology.

Archaeological finds and a significant number of Norse artifacts from Sweden have helped scholars piece together the stories of the gods and goddesses of the northlands. Huge burial mounds of ancient kings of Sweden—three located in Old Uppsala, about 50 miles north of Stockholm—have provided scientists with significant information about the Nordic people and their religious beliefs. Even farm fields in Sweden have been rich sources of information. Amulets, brooches, and stone carvings have been plowed up, uncovered, and preserved to provide information and greater understanding of the age of Norse mythology.

One of the richest sites of archaeological information is the Swedish island of GOTLAND, which lies in the Baltic Sea near the southern end of the peninsula. Here outlines of ships made with huge rocks still dot the landscape, and some of the most prominent rock carvings of ancient Scandinavia stand as reminders of this earlier age.

**SYN** (Refusal, Denial)  One of the ASYNJUR, or female goddesses. Syn guarded the door of FRIGG's great hall, SESSRUMNIR, keeping out all unwelcome visitors. Syn also was called upon to guide or protect defendants in trials.

# T

**TANNGNIOST** (Toothnasher) One of the two fierce billy goats that drew the cart of the god THOR. The other GOAT was TANNGRISNIR (Toothgrinder). To people on Earth, the rumble of the cart was heard as thunder. Thor's goats could be killed and eaten and then revived again the next day.

**TANNGRISNIR** (Toothgrinder) One of the two fierce billy goats that drew the cart of the god THOR. The other GOAT was TANNGNIOST (Toothgnasher). Thor's goats could be killed and eaten and then revived again the next day.

**THIALFI** Son of the farmer EGIL and brother of ROSKVA. He became THOR's servant because he had disobeyed Thor's command not to break any of the bones of the goats on which he and his family were feasting in "Thor's Journey to Utgard." Thialfi was long legged and fleet of foot, but he was outrun in a race with HUGI (Thought) in Utgard. Thialfi was also Thor's companion in the duel with the giant HRUNGNIR. He easily vanquished the clay giant, MOKKURKALFI, which the stone-headed giants had created in an attempt to frighten Thor.

**THIAZZI** (TJASSE, THJAZI) A powerful storm giant. He was the son of OLVALDI, brother of GANG and IDI, and father of SKADE. He lived in THRYMHEIM. Disguised as an EAGLE, Thiazzi tricked LOKI into helping him kidnap IDUNN, the goddess in charge of the magic apples of youth. In turn, Loki tricked the giant and returned Idunn to ASGARD. Thiazzi was killed at the gates of Asgard. His daughter, Skade, was given as a husband the VANIR god NIORD as compensation for her father's death. The great god ODIN threw Thiazzi's eyes into the heavens to stay there forever as gleaming stars.

**THOKK** (Coal) The giantess who refused to weep for BALDER, thus ensuring that he would remain in HEL's realm until RAGNAROK. Some mythologists believe that Thokk was LOKI, the trickster god, in disguise. Thokk personifies the darkness of the underground (where coal is formed) that will not weep for the light of the Sun (Balder).

**THOR** (Thunderer) The god of thunder and storms. His father was ODIN, his mother FJORGYN (1) (Earth). Thor had two wives: JARNSAXA (Ironstone), who bore him two sons, MODI and MAGNI; and golden-haired SIF, who gave him two daughters, LORA and THRUD (1). His realm was THRUDHEIM; his hall was BILSKIRNIR (Lightning), which had 540 rooms, fittingly large for this giant of a god who loved to feast and entertain. Thor was strong and fiery of temper, but he was well loved by the gods, respected by the GIANTS, and worshiped by the ordinary people.

Thor did not ride a horse; instead he had a chariot pulled by two enormous billy GOATs, TANNGNIOST and TANNGRISNIR. The wheels of the chariot made a noise like thunder when Thor raced across the heavens.

Thor's greatest possession was his hammer, MJOLLNIR. When he hurled it, the hammer always hit its mark and then returned to Thor like a boomerang. Mjollnir was not only a weapon but a symbol of fertility, used at weddings, and of resurrection, used at burials. Thor also had iron gauntlets with which he could crush rocks, and a belt, MEGINGJARDIR, which doubled his mighty strength.

At RAGNAROK, the end of the world, Thor killed JORMUNGAND, the Midgard Serpent, his ancient enemy, but himself was killed by the poisonous fumes of the dying serpent.

Worship of Thor continued for centuries after the coming of Christianity. The great OAK trees of central

Thor is shown here with his magic hammer, Mjollnir.
*(illustration by W. G. Collingwood, Anthony Mercatante)*

manliness. His hammer, Mjollnir, was a potent weapon, the gods' only real defense against the giants. Thor was seldom separated from his hammer, so it is not surprising that he went into a fury when the hammer disappeared.

LOKI, the trickster god, heard Thor's shouts and knew that for once he must be helpful rather than mischievous. He rushed to FREYA, the beautiful goddess, and borrowed her suit of FALCON feathers. Then Loki flew to JOTUNHEIM, the home of the giants.

THRYM, the huge and ugly king of the frost giants, was in a good mood, plaiting gold thread to make leashes for his colossal hounds. He greeted Loki cheerfully. Loki asked him if he had stolen Thor's hammer, and the giant admitted that he had. With a chilling laugh, he said that he had hidden it eight miles under the earth where no one would find it. The only way to get it back would be to send him Freya as his bride.

Even Loki was shocked at the thought of sending the fair goddess to this monster. Loki flew quickly back to ASGARD on his falcon wings and told Thor

and western Europe were sacred to the god. Worshipers of Thor made wooden oak chairs with high backs, called "high seats," to ensure Thor's blessing on the house (protecting it from lightning) and the well-being and fruitfulness of the family and its lands. As well as bringing thunder and lightning and storms, Thor sent the rain that made the fields fertile.

Evidence of Thor's popularity is found in the name Thursday (the fifth day of the week), and in numerous English place-names, such as Thundersley, in Essex; Thunderfield, Surrey; Thundridge, Hertfordshire; and many others in England and elsewhere.

There are many myths about Thor taken from the *POETIC EDDA* and the *PROSE EDDA*. In Richard WAGNER's opera *Der Ring des Nibelungen*, Thor appears as Donner. Thor is also found in Henry Wadsworth Longfellow's "Saga of King Olaf," part of *Tales of a Wayside Inn*.

The only source of the myth of the theft of Thor's hammer is the poem THRYMSKVITHA (*Lay of Thrym*) from the *Poetic Edda*. It is considered a masterpiece of burlesque.

**The Theft of Thor's Hammer**   Thor, the god of thunder, was the personification of strength and

Thor rode a chariot pulled by two billy goats. The wheels of the cart made a noise like thunder, and lightning flashed around them. *(Anthony Mercatante)*

the news. Together they went to Freya and told her of the giant's request.

Freya was so furious and agitated that she broke the clasp of her golden BRISINGAMEN. The starry beads scattered across the floor. Never, never would she be the bride of Thrym, she vowed.

Then all the gods got together for a meeting. They knew that it was only a matter of time until all the giants found out that Thor no longer had his hammer and would come marching on Asgard. The gods were worried.

Only HEIMDALL, the watchman who stood at BIFROST, the RAINBOW BRIDGE, and could see far into the future, remained calm. He said that Thor must be dressed as a bride and go to meet Thrym.

The gods roared with laughter at the thought of the mighty, red-bearded Thor dressed as a woman, and Thor let out a shout of rage. But gradually he saw the wisdom of the plan and allowed the goddesses to fit his large frame into a long dress and drape a veil over his shaggy head. Freya's necklace was repaired and placed around his thick neck, a girdle hung with jingling keys encircled his waist, and his manly chest was covered with glittering jewels.

Loki was dressed as a bridesmaid. Together the peculiar pair climbed into Thor's chariot, and the two billy goats took off at great speed, making the wheels rumble like thunder.

Thrym was overjoyed when he heard that Freya was on her way. He ordered the halls to be swept, new straw laid down, and a gargantuan feast prepared.

Thor was well known for his great appetite, but Thrym was astonished to see what he thought was a maiden eating such huge helpings of fish and meat and downing large goblets of MEAD. Quick-witted Loki explained that the bride had not eaten or drunk for eight days, so anxious was she to meet her groom.

Delighted, Thrym reached over to lift the bride's veil and kiss her, but when he saw Thor's flashing, red-rimmed eyes glaring at him through the veil, he fell back in dismay. Once again sly Loki whispered an explanation. The bride had not had a wink of sleep for eight nights, so anxious was she for her wedding night.

At that, Thrym ordered that the hammer be brought to his bride and the wedding ceremony commence at once, as it was the custom of the Norse to invoke the blessing of Thor's hammer at their wed-

dings. No sooner was Mjollnir placed upon his lap than Thor leapt up, tore off his veil, and started to slay every giant in sight.

**Thor and the Giant Geirrod**  The tale of how the god Thor destroyed the formidable giant GEIRROD and his two fearsome daughters is a popular myth, told several times in Norse literature, including in the SKALDSKAPARMAL in the *Prose Edda* and in SNORRI STURLUSON's retelling of *THORSDRAPA*.

One day Loki put on a suit of falcon feathers and flew to the hall of the giant Geirrod, one of the meanest of the JOTUNS. Geirrod caught sight of the handsome falcon and ordered the bird to be brought to him.

It took several of the trolls to capture Loki, for he hopped about the wall, always just out of reach. When at last he tried to take flight, he found himself stuck fast to the wall by some evil spell.

He was set before Geirrod, who knew at once that this was not a real falcon. He locked Loki in a cage and kept him without food and water until at last Loki confessed who he was. The giant set Loki free on the condition that he would bring him the thunder god, Thor, without any of his weapons. Faint with hunger, Loki agreed to bring Thor to Geirrod. Off he flew, his trickster's mind already devising a plan.

Once safe in Asgard, Loki prattled on to anyone who would listen about the wonders of Geirrod's castle and how the giant was eager to meet the mighty Thor, to introduce him to his two beautiful daughters, GIALP and GREIP, and to entertain him royally. Of course, Thor heard the gossip and, being a simple soul, could not long resist the temptation to visit Geirrod, his new admirer.

At Loki's urging, Thor left his weapons, even the magic hammer, Mjollnir, behind and set forth, with Loki at his side to show the way. As the distance was long, they stayed overnight with the kindly giantess GRID. She was friendly to the AESIR gods and liked Thor. When Loki had gone to sleep, she warned Thor about Geirrod and loaned him her belt of power, iron gloves, and magic staff.

The next day when Thor and Loki were crossing the rushing torrent of the VIMUR, the river began to rise higher and higher. Thor hung onto the magic staff, and Loki hung onto Thor, almost drowning in the blood-red river. Up ahead Thor saw the giantess

Gialp. It was she who was making the waters rise. Thor threw a rock at her, and she ran off, howling. Then Thor pulled himself to shore with the help of the small ROWAN tree, or mountain ash.

When they arrived at Geirrod's hall, Thor was shown into a small room. He sat down wearily in the only chair and closed his eyes. Suddenly he felt himself rising toward the roof. Quickly he rammed Grid's staff against the roof beam and pushed. Then down he came, right on top of Gialp and Greip, who had been trying to raise the chair and crush Thor against the roof. The two ugly, evil creatures were themselves crushed to death by Thor's weight.

Thor went straight to Geirrod. Geirrod shouted an ironic welcome, raising his hand in mock greeting and throwing a redhot lump of iron at Thor.

Thor caught it in Grid's iron gloves and threw it back at Geirrod, who leaped behind a pillar. The hot ball went right through the pillar, through Geirrod's head, and through the wall into the yard, where it bored deep into the earth. Thus Thor once more triumphed over treachery and guile—with the help of the giantess Grid.

**Thor's Journey to Utgard**  This story is one of the best known of the Norse myths. It is also one of the longest and most richly told myths written by Snorri in the *Prose Edda*, its only source.

One day the god Thor decided to go to UTGARD, stronghold of the largest giants in Jotunheim. Because its chief, UTGARD-LOKI, was known to be a master of trickery, Thor brought along Asgard's own trickster god, Loki.

As it grew dark Thor's chariot, drawn by two billy goats, stopped at a small farmhouse. The farmer and his wife were very poor and had little to eat. With a wave of his magic hammer, Mjollnir, Thor killed Tanngniost and Tanngrisnir, his goats, and put them on the fire to cook.

Thor told the peasants to eat their fill when the meat was ready but to be sure not to break any of the bones. They should be placed carefully onto the goatskins that Thor had stretched on the floor. THIALFI, the farmer's son, disobeyed Thor and cracked a leg bone to suck out the delicious marrow.

Next morning, when Thor was ready to leave, he waved Mjollnir over the piles of bone and skin and up sprang the goats, as lively as ever, but one of them

had a limp. Thor yelled in fury, for he knew that someone had disobeyed him. However, he accepted the terrified farmer's offer and took Thialfi and his sister, ROSKVA, to be his servants. He left the goats for the farmer to take care of until his return.

Thor and Loki and the two youngsters journeyed all day. That night they came to a forest in Jotunheim where the trees were so tall that their tops were lost in the clouds. They saw a strangely shaped cabin that seemed to have no door. They crept inside to shelter from the cold and were soon asleep.

In the middle of the night they sprang awake as the Earth shook, and there was a frightful crashing sound, followed by a steady rumble and a whistling wind. Even Thor was frightened. He, Loki, and the youngsters crept into a narrow side room in the cavernous hall, Thor clutching his hammer to his chest.

At first light, Thor went outside and saw the cause of all the noise. At the foot of a tree lay the biggest giant Thor had ever seen. He was fast asleep and snoring mightily.

Thor put on the magic belt given to him by the giantess Grid to double his strength. He held his hammer even more firmly, though the giant was so big that Thor decided not to throw it hastily.

Soon the giant woke up. He picked up what the travelers had mistaken for a large cabin or cave. It was a giant glove. The side room was the thumb.

When the giant stood up, Thor and his companions had to crane their heads back to look at him. The giant introduced himself as SKRYMIR, sometimes called Big Fellow or VASTY.

After they had eaten breakfast—a poor one for Thor and his friends, a huge one for Skrymir—they set off again, this time with the giant crashing through the trees ahead to show them the way to Utgard. By nightfall they were exhausted and hungry. The giant flung down his huge food bag, telling the other travelers to help themselves.

Try as they might, Thor, Loki and the farmer's son and daughter could not untie the knots that secured the bag, so they lay down, hungry, and tried to shut out the sound of Skrymir's thunderous snores.

At last Thor could not stand it any longer. He hit Skrymir on the head with his hammer. Skrymir opened one eye and complained that a leaf had fallen on his head. He was asleep again in a second.

Furious, Thor hit him again. Skrymir mumbled something about an acorn.

Beside himself, Thor took a running jump and hurled the hammer with all his might onto the giant's head. Skrymir finally sat up and rubbed his head. He decided that there must be some birds above his head. Skrymir got up and picked up his bag. He told the travelers to watch their step in Utgard, for the giants there were really big.

The four travelers breathed a sigh of relief as Skrymir lumbered off through the trees.

When they reached Utgard, the giants had assembled to meet them. They decided to engage in contests with the travelers.

Loki immediately announced that no one could beat him at eating. One of the giants placed a huge platter in front of Loki and sat down on the other side of it. The two began gobbling and in no time bumped heads as they met in the middle of the platter—or what was left of it. The giant had eaten his half of the wooden dish, along with all the bones, so he won the contest.

Next, young Thialfi claimed that he was the fastest runner in the world. Utgard-Loki called forth a young giant named HUGI, and marked out a racecourse.

Thialfi was indeed as swift as the wind, but he was no match for Hugi. Thialfi lost the race and retired to Loki's side, humiliated.

Thor strode forward, claiming that he was well known as a mighty drinker. The giants placed before him a long, curved horn. Confidently Thor took a huge drink, but when he looked at the horn, it was still brimming over with liquid. Once again he raised the horn to his lips. He opened his throat and let the liquid pour down until he was red in the face, but the horn was still almost full. After the third try, Thor put down the horn, mortified and angry.

Utgard-Loki shook his head sadly, remarking that the mighty Thor was not so mighty after all. Every one of his men could empty the horn at one draft. He suggested that Thor try his hand at something easier, like lifting a cat from the floor.

Grimly Thor put his hand under the cat's belly to lift it. It felt as heavy as a ton of lead. By using both his hands and all the strength of his mighty arms, he was able to raise the cat so that one paw was an inch off the floor. Then he fell back, exhausted.

Angry at the laughter of the giants, Thor shouted that he was the finest wrestler in all Asgard and would take on anyone.

The giant shook his head doubtfully. He could not think of a Jotun who would be bothered to fight such a weakling until he remembered his old foster mother, ELLI, and he summoned her to the hall.

Embarrassed, Thor put his hand out to grasp the arm of the skinny old crone, not meaning to hurt her. Suddenly he was flying through the air. He landed flat on his back. The wizened old woman cackled and the giants shouted with laughter. Then Thor wrestled the old woman in earnest, but no matter what he did the hag outplayed him, until at last he gave up and slunk away.

The next morning Utgard-Loki led the crestfallen travelers to the gates of Utgard. There, the giant admitted that he had practiced magic on them. First, he had disguised himself as Skrymir. He had used troll magic to tie the food bag with strands of iron. Then, when Thor thought he was hitting the giant's head with his hammer, he had been in fact hitting a hard rock. He told Thor that on his way home he would see the rock, a hillside with three very deep dents in it.

In the contests, too, he had used spells and trickery. LOGI, the giant who had beaten Loki in gluttony, was in fact Fire, which consumes everything in its path. The runner, Hugi, was Thought, and no one can move as fast as thought. The drinking horn was anchored in the seas of the world. No one can drain the oceans, but from then on, said the giant, the tides would ebb and flow, just as they had when Thor drank so mightily. Finally, the cat was Jormungand, the Midgard Serpent, who is so big that he encircles the world. When Thor had made the "cat" lift its paw, the serpent's back had almost touched the sky.

Thor was so angry at the trickery that he raised his hammer to strike the giant, but Utgard-Loki vanished into the air. So did the castle and its walls and all the other giants.

Although in this myth Thor is upstaged by Utgard-Loki, he is not totally humiliated, for he did create dents in the hillside and the ebbing and flowing of the tides.

**Thor and Hymir Go Fishing**   The myth of the fishing expedition of Thor and the giant HYMIR and Thor's battle with Jormungand, the Midgard Serpent,

In this picture, Thor grapples with the Midgard Serpent while the giant Hymir cringes in terror. *(New York Public Library Picture Collection)*

was a favorite and was retold many times, not only in SCANDINAVIA. In Gosforth, England, carvings on two stone slabs clearly show Thor fishing with an ox's head and fighting with the serpent. The *Lay of Hymir* is in *Hymiskvitha*, a poem of the *Poetic Edda*, and part of Snorri's *Prose Edda*.

The AESIR gods loved to eat and drink. No sooner was one feast over than they were making plans for the next. One evening they cast RUNES that told them that their next gathering should be at the abode of AEGIR, the Jotun lord of the sea. Aegir lived under the waves with his wife, RAN.

Aegir complained that he did not have a cauldron big enough to brew ale for all the gods. TYR, the one-handed god, declared that he knew where he could find a cauldron a mile deep. With Thor as his companion, Tyr set off to find Hymir, who lived east of ELIVAGAR in Jotunheim, the land of giants.

When they came to Hymir's dwelling, an ogress with 900 heads blocked their path, but there was another Jotun, beautiful and kind, and she welcomed Tyr as her son, and she welcomed Thor. She said she would try to help them and advised them to hide underneath the biggest cauldron in the hall.

Hymir lumbered into the hall, icicles dangling from his busy beard, and his eyes sparkling dangerously. He sensed the presence of strangers.

The Jotun woman explained that Tyr had come to visit and had brought a friend and that they were hiding under the big cauldron, being a little nervous of Hymir. Hymir's eyes swept the hall. At his ferocious glance pillars fell down and cauldrons shattered. But the biggest cauldron stayed whole, and Thor and Tyr crawled out unharmed.

Thor was an awesome sight, with his bristling red hair and beard. Hymir quickly ordered three oxen killed for their supper. Thor, who was famous for his huge appetite, ate two of the oxen. Hymir said that they would have to go hunting for the next meal. Thor suggested that they should fish for it instead.

For bait Thor took the head of a mighty black ox, HIMINBRIOTER (Skybellower). While Hymir rowed and caught a whale or two, Thor readied his tackle and cast his line into the water. Almost at once the terrible head of Jormungand, the Midgard Serpent, appeared above the waves, the ox's head in its mouth. Hymir's eyes bulged out in terror, but Thor coolly held the line and flung his hammer, Mjollnir, at the ghastly head. Again and again the hammer struck its mark and flew back to its master. Terrified, Hymir cut the line and the bloodied serpent sank beneath the waves.

Shaken, Hymir rowed back to the shore as fast as he could. Once safely on land, he decided to test Thor's strength. He asked him to either haul in the boat and tackle or carry the two whales up the cliff to the house. Without wasting a word, Thor took hold of the boat, dragged it out of the water and carried it, whales, and all to the house.

Tyr and the Jotun woman congratulated Thor on his feat of strength, but Hymir had yet another test for Thor. He handed him his goblet and asked Thor to try to break it. Thor hurled the goblet at the wall. Stone and rubble tumbled from the hole made in the wall, but the goblet remained intact.

Thor threw the goblet over and over again until the hall was in ruins. Then the giant's lovely wife whispered to him to throw the goblet at Hymir's head, which was the hardest object for miles around. Sure enough, when the goblet hit Hymir's stony head, it shattered into pieces, though the giant's head remained without a dent.

Then Hymir said that Thor could have the cauldron if he could carry it. Tyr tried to lift the cauldron but could not move it. Mighty Thor picked up the huge cauldron easily and wore it like a helmet. Then he and Tyr set off for home. On the way they were attacked by Hymir and many-headed Jotuns, but Thor wielded his magic hammer and put an end to Hymir and his ugly followers.

The Aesir gods drank deep from Hymir's cauldron in Aegir's halls for many a night to come.

**Thor's Duel with Hrungnir**  This story is from Snorri's *Prose Edda;* Snorri based his telling of this legend partly on the poem HAUSTLONG. The story of the god Thor's duel with the mighty giant HRUNGNIR begins with a horse race between Odin and the giant. On one of his journeys Odin, mounted on his eight-legged horse, SLEIPNIR, had met Hrungnir, the strongest of the giants. Hrungnir challenged Odin to a race on his splendid horse, GULLFAXI

Odin agreed and was off in a flash, with Hrungnir close behind. Sleipnir knew the way home well and streaked through VALGRIND, the gate of VALHALLA, Odin's hall.

Gullfaxi was going too fast to stop until he and his master were well within Asgard, the realm of the gods. The laws of hospitality dictated that the gods could not hurt their guest, Hrungnir.

The goddess FREYA gave Hrungnir Thor's great drinking horn and filled it to the brim. (Thor was away that day, fighting trolls in IRONWOOD.) Freya had to keep refilling the horn, for Hrungnir emptied it in huge gulps and soon became noisy and quarrelsome. He boasted that he would take all of Valhalla under his arm and carry it back to Jotunheim for a plaything. He would take Freya and golden-haired SIF, Thor's wife, to be his own wives and servants.

At this the gods grew angry, and Odin had a hard time keeping them from attacking their unpleasant guest. Just then Thor burst into the hall, brandishing Mjollnir, his hammer. He, too, wanted to attack the giant. Instead, he agreed to meet the giant at GIOTUNAGARD, the Place of Stones, to fight a duel.

Hrungnir clambered onto Gullfaxi and rode back to Jotunheim with the news. The giants were uneasy, even though Hrungnir was the strongest of them all. They put their heads together and came up with a plan. They would frighten Thor by making a huge clay giant, nine leagues high. They named the clay giant MOKKURKALFI and put inside it the heart of a mare, which was the biggest heart they could find.

Hrungnir's heart was made of stone, sharp-edged and three-cornered. His head, too, was made of stone, and so were his shield and club. Together, Mokkurkalfi and Hrungnir made a fearful sight as Thor and his servant, Thialfi, drew near.

Thialfi was quick witted as well as fleet of foot. He ran up to the giant and advised him to hold his shield low rather than high, in case Thor attacked him from below. The stone-headed giant flung his shield to the ground and stood on it with his big feet. Then he threw his club at Thor.

Thor threw his thunderbolt hammer at the giant's head at the same time. Club and hammer met in midair with an awesome crack and a sizzling bolt of lightning.

The giant's stone club shattered into a thousand pieces and fell to the earth, where to this day, it is said, the splinters may be found in quarries. But Thor's hammer zoomed on and struck the giant, who immediately fell dead. His outflung leg pinned Thor's head to the ground.

Thialfi, who had already hacked Mokkurkalfi to pieces, tried to release Thor, but the giant's leg was so huge and heavy that even when Odin and the other gods came to help, they could not move it an inch. Thor lay groaning, for a piece of Thialfi's club (made of WHETSTONE) was stuck in his head.

Along came Magni, Thor's son who was only three years old but already enormous. He lifted Hrungnir's leg easily, and Thor was at last able to roll free. Thor gave Magni Hrungnir's horse, Gullfaxi, as a reward.

Thor's head still hurt, so he sent for the clever witch, GROA. She cast some rune stones, and whispered some magic words, and the pain went away. Thor was so relieved that he wanted to make Groa happy. He told her that he had rescued her lost husband, AURVANDIL. He had carried him across the poisonous stream ELIVAGAR. Now Aurvandil was safe and waiting for Groa.

Groa was so happy at the news that she ran from the hall. In her excitement she forgot to cast a magic spell that would remove the stone from Thor's head.

Hrungnir was the strongest of Thor's adversaries, so the giants were uneasy about the outcome of the battle. With the defeat of Hrungnir, the war between the gods and the giants came to a turning point. Some mythologists believe that the giants now gave up hope of killing Thor and of storming Asgard.

**THORSDRAPA**  A late 10th-century poem by Eilif Guthrunarson. SNORRI STURLUSON included *Thorsdrapa* in his PROSE EDDA for an alternative version of the myth "Thor and the Giant Geirrod" (see under THOR).

**THRUD (1)** (Strength)  Most likely the daughter of the god THOR and his golden-haired wife, SIF. Little is known of Thrud, whose name survives in the KENNINGs, or metaphors, used by Old NORSE writers of SKALDIC POETRY. In one poem Thor is described as "father of Thrud." Scholars speculate from these kennings that the giant HRUNGNIR abducted Thrud, for he is referred to in one poem as the "thief of Thrud." As Thor's daughter, Thrud would be a half sister of MAGNI and of MODI and LORA's sister. Some experts also believe she is the person described in the *POETIC EDDA* as the betrothed to the DWARF ALVIS.

**THRUD (2)**   The name of one of the VALKYRIES who offers ale to the spirits of the dead warriors ODIN brings to live in VALHALLA.

**THRUDHEIM** (THRUDVANG; Place of Might) THOR's realm in ASGARD. It was the site of his huge hall, BILSKIRNIR.

**THRYM**   A HRIMTHURSSAR, or frost giant, sometimes called the king of the frost GIANTs. He stole THOR's hammer and demanded the goddess FREYA for his wife if the hammer was returned. With the help of the trickster LOKI, Thor won back the hammer at a wedding ceremony in which the thunder god posed as the bride. Once MJOLLNIR was in his possession Thor killed Thrym.

**THRYMHEIM** (Noisy Place)   The mountain home of the giant THIAZZI and his daughter, SKADE. It was a cold and lonely place, noisy with the howling of wind and of WOLF. In the story of "Skade and Niord," the god NIORD hated the place. The god LOKI came here to rescue IDUNN after she had been kidnapped by Thiazzi.

**THRYMSKVITHA** (*Lay of Thrym*)   A poem in the *POETIC EDDA* that is the only source of the story "The Theft of Thor's Hammer" (see under THOR).

**THUND** (Roaring)   The torrent or great river that flows just outside VALHALLA.

Thund is also one of the many names of the great god ODIN. It is included in *HAVAMAL*, one of the poems in the *POETIC EDDA*. SNORRI STURLUSON, the 13th-century author of the *PROSE EDDA*, included Thund in the list of Odin's names he recounts near the beginning of *GYLFAGINNING*, his major work on Norse mythology.

**THUNDER**   Thunder represented the power of nature and was an important part of many mythologies, including that of the Greeks. In Norse myths, THOR was known as the god of thunder, as well as of many other aspects of nature and life. This connection to the roar of thunder gave Thor a strong, power-

ful image, much like the pounding of the hammer of a blacksmith and the strength a man needed to swing such a hammer.

**THURSDAY**   The fifth day of the week, named after the god THOR.

**TREASURES OF THE DWARFS**   The story of how the gods came to acquire the treasures for which they were famed is one of the most popular of the Norse myths. It opens with the mischievous LOKI creeping into the bedroom of SIF, THOR's wife, and cutting off her golden hair while she sleeps.

When Thor discovered that Loki had cut off and stolen Sif's dazzling hair, Thor threatened to tear Loki into small pieces. The sly trickster put on a fine show of remorse and promised to bring back not only hair made of real gold for Sif, but other treasures as well, so Thor let him go.

Loki immediately made his way to SVART-ALFHEIM, the underworld caverns where the DWARFS lived. These misshapen, undersized creatures were ugly and bad-tempered, but they were master craftsmen when it came to mining and shaping gold and the other metals found in their darkling realm.

Loki went first to the cave of the sons of Ivaldi. He begged them to make golden strands so real that they would grow out of Sif's head. This feat the dwarfs accomplished with their magic, and while the furnace was still hot they made other magical treasures for Loki to carry home to the gods.

*SKIDBLADNIR* was a marvelous ship for FREY. It could fold up small enough to fit into a pouch and yet expand to a size large enough to carry all the AESIR gods and their equipment. It could sail on land or sea or air.

For ODIN they made GUNGNIR, a strong and slender spear that always flew straight to its target.

On his way home Loki stopped at the cave of BROKK and EITRI. These two dwarfs wanted to show that their work was much finer than that of the sons of Ivaldi. Loki was happy to let them try. The more treasures he retrieved from the gods, the more they would feel like forgiving him for all his mischief. Loki bet his head that Brokk and Eitri could not do better work than the Ivaldi brothers.

Then, in spite of Loki's teasing (he turned himself into a gadfly and kept stinging poor Brokk as he pumped the bellows), the dwarfs made GULLINBRUSTI, a BOAR with bristles and mane of shining gold, which Loki gave to Frey, and DRAUPNIR, an arm ring of gold that, on every ninth night, dropped eight more rings just as beautiful as the first. Draupnir became Odin's favorite arm ring.

Finally the dwarfs produced MJOLLNIR, a massive iron hammer. The hammer had a short handle because Loki, as a gadfly, had made Brokk pause for an instant at the bellows, causing the fire to cool. Nonetheless, the hammer had the magic property of always reaching its mark and then returning at once to its owner, Thor.

When Loki presented the treasures, the gods agreed that the wondrous hammer was the most powerful treasure of all, for it could guard the gods against the giants.

Brokk claimed that he was the winner of the bet and that Loki owed him his head, but as usual, Loki used fast talk and cunning and escaped with nothing worse than sore lips when Brokk tried to sew up his wicked mouth.

Sif was delighted with her new growth of precious gold hair. The term *Sif's hair* was used in Norse myths as a KENNING, or condensed metaphor, for "gold."

This story plays an important part in the Norse myths, for it makes clear the origins of the associations such as Thor and his hammer and Odin and his spear that had existed for as long as the gods had been known in SCANDINAVIA.

**TUESDAY**   The third day of the week. It is named after the one-handed war god, TYR.

**TYR** (TIW, TIV, ZIV)   A god of war and the sky god, the bravest of all the gods. He was concerned with justice and with fair treaties. It is thought that at one time Tyr was even more important than ODIN, and more ancient. By the time the Norse myths were written down, Tyr's importance had diminished, and not much is known about him. In some stories, Tyr is the son of the giant HYMIR; in others he is the son of Odin.

Of all the gods, Tyr was the only one brave enough to feed Fenrir, the monster wolf. *(Anthony Mercatante)*

Tyr was the only god brave enough and fairminded enough to put his hand into the jaws of the terrible WOLF FENRIR. When the other gods broke their word to Fenrir and tied him up, Fenrir bit off Tyr's hand. That is why Tyr is always depicted as the one-handed god.

At RAGNAROK, the end of the world, Tyr and GARM, Hel's hound, killed each other.

Tuesday (in Old English *Tiwesdaeg*) was named after Tyr.

**ULL** (ULLER)  The winter god of skiers and of hunting, snowshoes, the bow, and the shield. Son of the goddess SIF and stepson of THOR, Ull lived in YDALIR.

In NORSE poetry, a shield is often referred to as "Ull's ship." Scholars believe this reference means that Ull may have skied down hills on his shield much as one might use a modern-day snowboard.

SAXO GRAMMATICUS, the 13th-century Danish historian, refers to Ull as a cunning magician and says that Ull traveled over the sea on a magic bone. Archaeologists have found skates made of bones in ancient Scandinavian sites and suggest that it was to these that Saxo was referring.

Though the Norse authors, including 13th-century Icelandic writer SNORRI STURLUSON, wrote very little about Ull, he appears from other evidence to have been a very important god to the Norse people.

**URD** (WYRD; Past)  One of the three NORNS, or Fates, who spun on their web the destiny of all living beings. Urd was the most powerful of the three. The sacred Well of Urd (URDARBRUNN) was named after her. She is the oldest of the three sisters and is usually pictured as looking backward.

**URDARBRUNN** (Well of Urd, Well of Fate)  The well or spring at the center of ASGARD, which was the home of the AESIR gods.

Urdarbrunn was a powerful symbol in Norse mythology. Its waters flowed out at the base of one of the three great roots of YGGDRASIL, the World Tree. The well was named after URD, one of the NORNS, or Fates, who determined the directions of people's lives. Based on the well's name, scholars argue that the NORSE people believed the waters of this well contained great powers.

The gods rode their horses to this well each day and sat there in judgment over the world.

**UTGARD** (Outer Place)  The capital of JOTUNHEIM, the land of the GIANTS, according to SNORRI STURLUSON. The stronghold was ruled by the giant king SKRYMIR, or UTGARD-LOKI. The god THOR was humiliated and defeated in Utgard by the magic of the giant king.

**UTGARD-LOKI** (Loki of the Outer World)  The strongest and most cunning of the GIANTS. Also known as SKRYMIR, he humiliated and outwitted the gods THOR and LOKI and their servant THIALFI in the story "Thor's Journey to Utgard."

**VAFTHRUDNISMAL** (*Vafthrudnir; Lay of Vaf-thrudnir*) A 10th-century poem from the *POETIC EDDA*. Vafthrudnir is described as a "wise giant and riddle master." ODIN, using the name Gagnrad, visits the giant to test his knowledge and to obtain some wisdom. The poem takes the form of a question-and-answer game between Odin and the giant. (This format was common in the Eddic poems.)

First Odin answers Vafthrudnir's questions. The giant is impressed by his guest's knowledge and in turn answers Odin's questions about the Sun and the Moon, day and night, winter and summer, the first GIANTS, the VANIR gods, the hall of dead heroes, and the fate of the gods. Finally Odin asks about the end of the world and the world thereafter. Odin in turn is impressed by the giant's knowledge and asks him how he acquired it. Vafthrudnir says that he has roamed far and wide, even to the home of the dead in NIFL-HEIM, and can also read the RUNES.

The *Lay of Vafthrudnir* is a valuable source of information about the Norse myths. All of it appears in the *CODEX REGIUS* and some of it in the *Arnamagnean Codex* of the *Poetic Edda*. SNORRI STURLUSON draws upon it extensively in the *PROSE EDDA*.

**VALASKIALF** The great god ODIN's silver-roofed hall in ASGARD, the home of the gods. It was the site of HLIDSKIALF, the high seat from which Odin could observe all NINE WORLDS.

**VALGRIND** (Death's Gate) The outer gate of VALHALLA, the hall of the slain.

**VALHALLA** (Hall of the Slain) The hall built by the god ODIN in ASGARD to receive heroes slain in battle. The warriors, called EINHERJAR, fought all day and feasted all night. They were brought to Valhalla by the VALKYRIES, Odin's warrior maidens, led by the goddess FREYA. The heroes went to battle at Odin's side at RAGNAROK, the end of the world, in which all were slain once again.

In modern English the word *Valhalla* means "a heavenly place where the deserving dead find eternal happiness, or an esteemed burial place on earth."

Valhalla appears in the *POETIC EDDA* (especially in GRIMNISMAL) and SNORRI STURLUSON's *PROSE EDDA*.

**The Hall of Dead Heroes** Odin, the ALFODR and warrior god of the AESIR, built Valhalla, the Hall of the slain. It was situated in GLADSHEIM, Odin's realm in Asgard. It was splendid indeed, the most beautiful hall there. The roof was tiled with shining shields, the rafters were flashing spears, and on the benches were fine suits of armor, ready for the warriors to put on. There Odin planned to receive all the brave men who had died as heroes on Earth and give them everlasting life so that they could help the gods fight the GIANTS at Ragnarok, the end of the world.

The Valkyries, Odin's splendid warrior maidens (some were his daughters), put on their gleaming armor and went down to MIDGARD, or Middle Earth, to choose which warriors were brave enough and strong enough to be rewarded with a new life in Valhalla. They returned with the heroes, or Einherjar, who had been slain in battle but were now miraculously alive, their wounds healed and their health robust.

The maidens donned white robes and poured MEAD from drinking horns into the soldiers' goblets, the bony skulls of their stricken enemies. The supply of mead never ended, for it came from the enchanted she-GOAT HEIDRUN, who nibbled on the leaves of LAERAD, the tree around which the hall was built.

The food was abundant, too. It came from another magical creature, the BOAR SAEHRIMNIR. Each night

These carvings from stones in Gotland, Sweden, show warriors raising their drinking horns (left) and the roasting of the boar in Valhalla. *(New York Public Library Picture Collection)*

Saehrimnir was killed, cooked, and eaten by the hungry heroes. Each morning the boar rose up again, ready to go through the whole ritual again. The heroes never went hungry or thirsty, despite their enormous appetites, and Odin looked on with approval.

Odin bade the warriors put on the shining new armor and find the horses in the courtyard. They could fight all day to their hearts' content. If they were wounded, they would be healed. If they were killed, they would come back to life again, ready to enjoy another night of feasting.

And so it was that Odin gradually built up a vast army, 800 strong, of the world's best warriors, who would march out of the 540 doors of Valhalla and valiantly fight beside Odin and the Aesir gods at Ragnarok.

**VALI (1)**   The son of LOKI and SIGYN and the brother of NARFI. In "Loki's Punishment," after the gods capture Loki, they turn Vali into a WOLF who tears out the entrails of Narfi. The gods use the entrails to bind Loki.

**VALI (2)**   The youngest son of the god ODIN. His mother was RINDA. Vali avenged BALDER's death by slaying the blind god HODUR with his arrow. He was one of the few gods to survive RAGNAROK, the end of the world.

Vali is a personification of the light of the days that grow longer as spring approaches. Because rays of light were often depicted as arrows, Vali was usually represented and worshiped as an archer. For that reason his month in old Norwegian calendars is designated by the sign of the bow and is called Lios-beri, the "light bringer." Lios-beri falls between the modern calendar's mid-January and mid-February.

**Vali, the Avenger**   Vali was the youngest son of the god ODIN. This myth tells of Vali's origins and of how he avenged the death of his half brother, Balder. It is part of "Balder's Dream" in the POETIC EDDA.

When Balder, Odin's beloved son, began having frightening dreams, Odin made a journey to the underworld to seek the knowledge of an ancient sybil. She told Odin that Balder would be killed and that his death would be avenged by another son of Odin's, Vali, as yet unborn. The child's mother would be Rinda. Vali would slay Hodur (Balder's killer) when he was but one night old, with his hands still unwashed and his hair uncombed.

Odin next sent HERMOD, the messenger of the gods, to the wicked but powerful wizard ROSTIOFF, in Lapland, to find out more. Hermod took Odin's horse, SLEIPNIR, and runic spear, and set off. The journey was long and there were many perils, but at last Hermod reached the desolate country where the wizard dwelled. Rostioff was not welcoming. He took the form of a terrible giant and approached Hermod with a strong rope, but Hermod struck him with the magic staff, and the giant fell at once. Hermod bound Rostioff with his own rope.

The wizard promised to help Hermod if he could be freed from the rope. Hermod loosened the ties. Rostioff chanted spells until the sky grew dark; then the sky reddened into a vision of blood—the blood of Balder. Out of it rose a beautiful woman with a boy-child in her arms. The boy leaped to the ground and immediately started to grow into a man. He shot an arrow into the gloom and then the vision disappeared.

The wizard explained that the woman was Rinda, daughter of King BILLING of the Ruthenians. She was to be the mother of Vali, who would slay Hodur with his bow and arrow. Hermod took the news back to Odin.

Then Odin disguised himself as an ordinary man and set off to find and win Rinda. He easily won favor with King Billing, but beautiful Rinda was strong headed and resisted Odin through many of his cleverest disguises. He won her in the end by using magic RUNES, and she agreed to marry him.

Nine months later Vali, a newborn with hands as yet unwashed and hair uncombed, walked over BIFROST into ASGARD. To everyone's amazement he started to grow and grow, until he was as big as a man. Odin realized that the boy was his son Vali. Vali drew an arrow from the quiver that he would always carry and shot it at Hodur, who died instantly, and Balder's death was avenged.

Vali became one of the youngest warrior gods, a god of light, and was one of the few to survive Ragnarok.

**VALKYRIES** (Choosers of the Slain) Warrior maidens of the god ODIN. They chose men doomed to die in battle and delivered them to Odin's VALHALLA (Hall of the Slain). There the resurrected heroes enjoyed a life of unending feasting and fighting, preparing for RAGNAROK, the end of the world.

The maidens went down to MIDGARD in full armor, their golden hair flying from underneath their winged helmets. They would hover over the chosen warriors in the thick of battle. When a hero fell dead or mortally wounded, a Valkyrie would sweep him up and carry him on horseback to ASGARD, where the gods lived.

The Valkyries had such names as Shrieker and Screamer, Storm Raiser, Axe Time, Spear Bearer, Shield Bearer, Mist, and others. The number of Valkyries varied between six, nine, and 13 at a time.

In some stories FREYA herself was the goddess-leader of the Valkyries. She was allowed to choose warriors to be entertained in her hall, SESSRUMNIR, in her realm, FOLKVANGER, instead of sending them to Odin's Valhalla.

In Valhalla, the Valkyrie maidens would don graceful gowns and serve the EINHERJAR (slain heroes) with food and drink.

Most of the maidens were from Asgard, daughters of the gods and goddesses. Some were Odin's daughters. Odin allowed some of the maidens to take the form of beautiful white swans, but if a Valkyrie was seen by a human without her swanlike disguise, she would become an ordinary mortal and could never again return to Valhalla.

The German composer Richard WAGNER wrote an opera *The Valkyries (Die Walküre)* as part of the

The Valkyries, Odin's warrior maidens, carried dead heroes to Valhalla. *(Anthony Mercatante)*

*Ring des Nibelungen* cycle. It was first performed in Munich in 1870. In it Brunhilda is chief of the Valkyries. Wagner's "Ride of the Valkyries" is cited as one of the most stirring pieces of 19th-century orchestral music.

**VANAHEIM (VANALAND)** The realm or kingdom of the VANIR, the gods of the earth, fertility, and plenty. This realm was neighbor to ASGARD, home of the AESIR gods. After the great WAR BETWEEN THE AESIR AND THE VANIR, ODIN, the greatest of the Aesir, sent the gods HOENIR and MIMIR to Vanaheim, and the Vanir sent NIORD, FREY, and FREYA to Asgard.

Vanaheim also refers to the Tanais, an ancient NAME for the Don River in western Russia.

**VANIR** A race of gods and goddesses who lived in VANAHEIM. They were the original gods, more ancient than the AESIR. They were gods of fertility. Chief among them were the twin deities FREY and FREYA. After the war with the Aesir (see WAR BETWEEN THE AESIR AND THE VANIR), Frey, Freya, and their father, NIORD, and possibly HEIMDALL went to live in ASGARD, home of the Aesir. After that war all the gods were referred to as Aesir.

The Vanir gods brought peace and plenty to Asgard. They also brought their knowledge of SEID, magic and witchcraft, and instructed the Aesir in its practice. The Vanir were worshiped for centuries in northern lands.

**VAR (Pledge)** A goddess, one of the ASYNJUR, or females among the AESIR gods. Var's special responsibility was to hear the oaths and vows of faithfulness made between men and women and to punish those who broke those vows. THOR calls upon Var's power when he, dressed up as FREYA, pretended to marry the giant THRYM in the Old NORSE poem *THRYMSKVITHA*.

**VASTY** The giant SKRYMIR. Vasty is the name used for the giant in some English retellings of the myth, particularly those intended for young readers.

**VE** According to SNORRI STURLUSON in GYLFAGIN-NING, one of ODIN's brothers, along with VILI; son of BOR and the giantess BESTLA. Together the three sons of Bor created the Earth and the heavens from the body of the giant YMIR and the first HUMANS from the trunks of two trees. In Snorri's version of the CREATION story of Norse mythology, it was Ve who gave the humans warmth and color.

In the *VOLUSPA* the three sons of Bor are called Odin, HOENIR (VILI), and LOTHUR (Ve).

**VEGTAM (Wanderer)** The name used by the god ODIN when he went to visit VOLVA. Claiming to be the son of Valtam, Odin went to her to seek help for his beloved son BALDER.

**VERDANDE (Present)** One of the three NORNS, or Fates. She is usually pictured as looking straight ahead.

**VESTRI (WESTRI; West)** One of the four DWARFS who represented the four main compass points. The others are AUSTRI (East), NORDI (North), and SUDRI (South). Though these dwarfs are mentioned in early NORSE poetry, only 13th-century Icelandic writer SNORRI STURLUSON assigned to them the job of holding up the four corners of the sky.

**VIDAR** Son of the god ODIN and the kindly giantess GRID. His home was called VIDI (or Landvidi), a place of tall grasses, wildflowers, and growing saplings, a silent and peaceful place. Vidar, too, was known for his silence, but it was he who would avenge his father's death at RAGNAROK, the end of the world. On that day Vidar leaped from his horse and attacked the WOLF FENRIR, who had devoured Odin. Vidi placed one foot on the beast's lower jaw and pushed on the upper jaw with his hands until the monster was torn in two.

Legend has it that Vidar wore a special shoe or boot that had been made from the scraps that cobblers had saved over the years as they trimmed the leather they used for shoes. Another story says that Grid made the shoe for Vidar.

Vidar was one of the few gods who survived Ragnarok and became one of the rulers of the new world.

A famous stone at Gosforth Church, in Cumbria, England, shows Vidar fighting with Fenrir.

**VIDFINN (Wood-Finn)** The human father of the children BIL AND YUKI, who were stolen to serve MANI, the man in the Moon. Vidfinn sent his children to the well BYRGIR for water. Along the journey Mani stole the children and put them to work on the Moon.

Only SNORRI STURLUSON mentions Vidfinn. Some scholars suggest that the name Vidfinn is Finnish and that Snorri or his sources wanted to connect this father and his children with a land they thought to be very distant from SCANDINAVIA.

**VIDI** The home of the god VIDAR. It was a silent and peaceful place, full of grasses, flowers, and saplings. It was sometimes called Landvidi.

**VIGRID** (VIGRITH; Field of Battle) The immense plain, stretching 120 leagues in every direction, on which the bloody battle of RAGNAROK was fought.

**VIKINGS** (People of the Inlets) Scandinavian warriors who raided the coasts and inlets of Europe and the British Isles from the ninth to the 12th centuries (the Viking Age). Their greatest achievements were in shipbuilding and navigation (see SHIPS AND SHIP BURIALS). The typical longship was a graceful vessel with a high prow adorned with the figure of an animal, often a dragon, and a high curved stern. It had a square sail and was powered by oarsmen who hung their shields over the side of the ship. They ventured as far away as Greenland, ICELAND and North America, and founded colonies in NORWAY, DENMARK, and SWEDEN, as well as in the British Isles, around the Mediterranean, in Russia, and in North America.

Their mythological and heroic legends form the content of Old NORSE literature. The Viking Age ended, however, in the 12th century with the coming of Christianity to SCANDINAVIA and the rise of European states, whose people were able to join together and protect themselves against further Viking invasions and raids. Many Vikings settled down in the lands that they had raided. They came to be known by the names of the new states: Danes, Norse, Swedes, Normans, and Varangians (in Russia).

In spite of their reputation for ferocity, not all Vikings were warriors. Most of them were farmers, hunters, and fishermen who led peaceful lives and had a stable social structure. Family and social bonds were vital, for many communities were small and

A Viking warrior *(New York Public Library Picture Collection)*

The prow of the Viking longship was often adorned with the head of a dragon. *(New York Public Library Picture Collection)*

isolated, especially in the middle of the dark, grim northern winters. The literature that has come down to us from the Vikings shows that they had a strong streak of humor, common sense, and fairness. They were a brave people, acknowledging that life can be hard and that death will come to all, but it is to be met bravely and without complaint. The poem RIGSTHULA gives us a detailed picture of how people lived in the Viking Age.

**VILI** According to SNORRI STURLUSON in GYLFAGINNING, one of ODIN's brothers, along with VE; son of BOR and the giantess BESTLA. Together the three sons of Bor created the Earth and the heavens from the body of the giant YMIR and the first HUMANS from the trunks of two trees. In Snorri's version of the CREATION story of Norse mythology, it was Vili who gave the humans their senses and the ability to move.

In the *VOLUSPA* the three sons of Bor are named Odin, HOENIR (Vili), and LOTHUR (Ve).

**VIMUR** A rushing river in JOTUNHEIM. The giantess GIALP tried to raise the level of the torrent, some translations say by urinating in the river, to drown the god THOR, but Thor hit her with a well-aimed stone and she ran off, howling.

**VINGOLF** (Friendly Floor, Friend Hall) Possibly the mansion home of the goddess FRIGG and the other ASYNJUR. Vingolf stood in ASGARD, home of the AESIR, next to GLADSHEIM, the palace that contained the thrones of ODIN and the other 12 main gods.

SNORRI STURLUSON wrote in his *PROSE EDDA* that Vingolf is another name for VALHALLA, the palace that Odin built in Asgard as a dwelling for human heroes who died in battle.

**VOLSUNGA SAGA** A late 13th-century prose epic, telling of the hero SIGURD (called Siegfried in German), youngest son of Volsung. Volsung was a descendant of the god ODIN. The myth "Otr's Ransom" (see under OTR) and the legends of Sigurd are from the *Volsunga*. Richard WAGNER based his opera cycle *Der Ring des Nibelung* in part on the *Volsunga*.

**VOLUSPA** (*The Sibyl's Prophecy*) A NORSE poem from ICELAND, recorded in the late 10th or early 11th century. It is perhaps the most important poem in the *POETIC EDDA*. The poem takes the form of a monologue delivered by the VOLVA, or sibyl, in answer to ODIN's questions. (The question-and-answer format was common in Eddic poems.) The verses deal with the CREATION of the world, of the gods and of HUMANS; tell of the WAR BETWEEN THE AESIR AND THE VANIR; and recount the death of BALDER and LOKI's punishment. They also tell of Loki's monstrous children, FENRIR, the WOLF, and JORMUNGAND, the Midgard Serpent, and the part they played at RAGNAROK, the end of the world. At the end of the poem the new world begins, a kind of green paradise in GIMLÉ, marred only by the presence of the corpse-eating dragon NITHOG. Many scholars believe that the *Voluspa* is one of the greatest literary achievements in the Norse world.

**VOLVA** (VALA) A seeress or soothsayer; a kind of magician, usually female, able to see into the future and remember from the past, and capable of giving advice to the living who call her up from the grave for consultations.

In the myth of BALDER, ODIN goes to the underworld to consult the Volva to try to learn the reason for his son Balder's frightening dreams. Odin learns from the Volva that his son will die.

In the *SVIPDAGSMAL*, Svipdag calls up the spirit of his mother, GROA, to ask her advice in the wooing of the fair MENGLOD.

The goddess FREYA is associated with the Volvas, but no stories survive that describe her role as seeress.

**VOR** (Wary, Careful) One of the ASYNJUR, or goddesses of the AESIR, according to SNORRI STURLUSON in his *PROSE EDDA*. Other existing manuscripts also mention Vor but do not specify that she was a goddess. They do, however, say that she was very wise and searched out all things so that nothing was hidden from her. She had the gift of providence, of preparing well for the future.

**WAGNER, RICHARD** (1813–1883) German composer of operas who drew heavily on German and Norse mythology for his stories. Wagner based his series of four operas known as *Der Ring des Nibelungen* on a 13th-century German poem and the NORSE stories in the *VOLSUNGA SAGA*, the *POETIC EDDA*, and the *PROSE EDDA*.

**WAR BETWEEN THE AESIR AND THE VANIR** The AESIR were the warrior gods who lived in ASGARD. The VANIR gods existed long before the first Aesir gods appeared. They were beautiful beings of light and wisdom who lived in their realm called VANAHEIM, sending forth gentle sunshine and rain and fertility. They never set foot in Asgard, nor did they seem to know of the existence of the Aesir.

One day, according to some tellings of this story, a beautiful witch named GULLWEIG or HEID appeared in Asgard, and the seeds were sown for a battle between the Aesir and the Vanir, the very first war. Gullweig had a great hunger for gold. She could never have enough. She talked about it constantly, disturbing the gods. Wickedness had come to Asgard. The great god, ODIN, was very angry and decided that the witch must die.

Three times the Aesir cast Gullweig into the fire, and three times she rose up, more beautiful than ever. She went into every hall in Asgard, casting spells and teaching magic.

Then Gullweig went to the Vanir and told them how cruelly she had been treated by the Aesir. Soon an army of Vanir, perhaps led by brave NIORD, appeared at the walls of Asgard, ready to avenge Gullweig. Odin cast his spear, GUNGNIR, and the battle raged until both armies grew tired of the slaughter. It seemed that neither side could win—or lose.

The leaders of the Aesir and the Vanir got together to discuss terms. In the end they agreed that there should be eternal peace between them and that together they would stand fast against the common enemy, the GIANTS.

To seal the peace treaty, the Aesir and the Vanir spat into a jar, as was the custom of the Northmen when making treaties. From the spittle formed KVASIR, the wisest of the wise (see "The Mead of Poetry," under ODIN).

As a sign of good faith, the sides exchanged gods. Odin sent his brother HOENIR and the wise god MIMIR to live among the Vanir. And Niord and his son and daughter, FREY and FREYA, settled in Asgard.

At first the Vanir were delighted with the handsome Hoenir. They made him one of their leaders, but they soon noticed that Hoenir could make no decisions unless he consulted Mimir. They felt that the Aesir had cheated them. They did not dare harm Odin's brother, however, so they cut off Mimir's head and sent it back to Odin. Odin immediately used his magic to restore the head to life. He placed it in a spring, known as MIMIR'S WELL, at the foot of the sacred tree, YGGDRASIL, and he regularly went to seek its wisdom.

According to some scholars, this myth may represent folk memory of the conflict between the adherents of two different cults, which were then brought together. After the conflict, the Aesir win control of the embodiment of wisdom and inspiration—Kvasir—in one myth, and the head of Mimir in another, they learn the magic of the Vanir, and all the gods are now referred to as Aesir.

**WATCHMAN OF THE GODS** The title and task assigned to HEIMDALL, one of the AESIR gods. According to NORSE beliefs, the post of guardian was considered very important. As watchman, Heimdall sat at the edge of heaven and protected the Aesir from the GIANTS. He also watched for events marking the beginning of the end of time, known as RAGNAROK, the battle between the gods and the giants. Heimdall warned the gods when the battle was about to begin.

## WESTRI See VESTRI.

## WHETSTONE
A stone used for sharpening tools. The stone is often quartz because of the hardness and sharpness of its broken grains. In Norse mythology whetstones were made from the pieces of the giant HRUNGNIR's club, which shattered when it was hit by THOR's hammer. In the story "Thor's Duel with Hrungnir," some pieces of whetstone lodged in Thor's head, giving him a headache whenever whetstones were carelessly moved or dropped near him.

In the story of how the great god ODIN obtained the MEAD of poetry, Odin uses a whetstone to sharpen the workers' tools. The workers are so eager to have the whetstone that they kill each other with their sharpened weapons in a wild scramble.

At the Sutton Hoo ship burial in England, an impressive whetstone, thought to be a scepter, was found in a seventh-century grave (see SHIPS AND SHIP BURIALS).

## WOLF
Wolves were both friends and enemies of the gods in Norse mythology. They were companions of the great god ODIN, for example, who fed GERI and FREKI table scraps at VALHALLA. These wolves roamed throughout the great hall, walking among the souls of human warriors. HUMANS in battle, therefore, considered wolves to be signs of Odin's presence. A gray wolf on the battlefield was a positive sign to warriors, for they believed it would guide their spirits to Valhalla if they died in the battle.

More often, however, wolves were vicious enemies of the gods. Wolves chased the SUN AND MOON across the sky, threatening with growls and gnashing teeth to devour both, which they finally did at RAGNAROK, the ultimate conflict between the gods and the GIANTS. The gods turned VALI (1), a son of the trickster god, LOKI, into a wolf that then tore to pieces his brother NARFI. The gods then converted Narfi's entrails to iron and used them to bind Loki.

The most powerful wolf, the giant FENRIR, also a son of Loki, threatened the very existence of the gods. They eventually succeeded in chaining him as a captive, but at Ragnarok he broke free. Scholars see the binding of Fenrir as a symbolic attempt to protect humankind from this enemy of nature.

# Y

**YDALIR** (Yew Dales) The valleys where YEW trees grow. The home of ULL, the winter god of skiers, snowshoes, and hunting.

**YEW** An evergreen tree of the family Taxaceae. In ancient belief systems the European yew (*Taxus baccata*) was thought to have magic properties. In Norse mythology YDALIR (Yew Dales) was the home of the winter god ULL.

**YGGDRASIL** The ASH tree of Norse myth, called the World Tree because it forms a link between the NINE WORLDS.

At the uppermost level are ASGARD, home of the AESIR gods; VANAHEIM, home of the VANIR gods; and ALFHEIM, home of the light ELVES.

On the next level lie MIDGARD (Earth), the home of HUMANS; JOTUNHEIM, home of the JOTUNS, or GIANTS; SVARTALFHEIM, home of the dark elves; and NIDAVELLIR, home of the DWARFS.

In the dark underworld, Yggdrasil's roots reach MUSPELLHEIM, land of fire, and NIFLHEIM, including HEL's realm, the land of the dead.

Three wells water the roots of Yggdrasil. One is the Well of URD, URDARBRUNN, a sacred place tended by the three NORNS and where the gods sit in council.

The second is MIMIR'S WELL, in which is preserved the head of the wisest of all beings, MIMIR. ODIN himself consults Mimir when in need of knowledge.

The third spring is Vergelmir, in Niflheim, the land of the dead. The foul dragon NITHOG lives there, forever nibbling at the roots of Yggdrasil.

Writhing serpents breathe clouds of venom onto the roots of Yggdrasil. Huge stags and GOATS tear leaves and bark from the tree. Yggdrasil survives all these torments, helped by the Norns who sprinkle Urd's water upon the roots. It will survive RAGNAROK,

the end of the world, though it will tremble. LIF and LIFTHRASIR will hide in the depths of the tree, fed on its dew and emerge afterward to repeople the earth.

In the topmost branches of Yggdrasil sits a mighty EAGLE with a small hawk upon its brow, surveying the world. A squirrel, RATATOSK, scampers up and down the tree bearing tales from Nithog to the eagle and back again.

Once Odin hanged himself from the branches of Yggdrasil for nine nights to learn the secret of the RUNES. The Norse sometimes called the gallows a horse (*drasil*), and Odin, Ygg (Terrible One).

A tree is commonly used in myths to symbolize long life, fertility, regeneration, and knowledge.

**YMIR** (Confused Noise) The first giant, or JOTUN. He was formed from ice and fire at the beginning of time in the vast chasm of GINNUNGAGAP, which lay between icy NIFLHEIM and fiery MUSPELLHEIM. Ymir was nourished by the first cow, AUDHUMLA, and he grew to a huge size.

As Ymir slept, male and female GIANTS sprang from his armpits, and from his feet grew a sixheaded troll. From these creatures began the HRIMTHURSSAR, the race of frost giants, all huge and hideously ugly.

After the first gods, ODIN, VILI, and VE, were born from BOR and BESTLA, the gods quarreled constantly with the giants and at last killed Ymir.

From Ymir's body the gods created MIDGARD, the Middle Earth. Ymir's blood formed the seas and all the lakes and rivers. His flesh became the hills and plains, his bones the mountains and his teeth the rocks. His hair formed trees and all vegetation.

The gods placed Ymir's skull as a dome over the earth, and his brains they cast to the winds to become clouds.

See also CREATION.

**YNGVI** Another name, or perhaps title, for the god FREY; also possibly a little-known son of ODIN.

This name is sometimes joined with Frey, as in Yngvi-Frey, in the poetry and legends of Norse mythology. SNORRI STURLUSON, the author of the PROSE EDDA, explained that Yngvi was a term of respect used to refer to this particular god.

Yngvi, like ING, is used in NORSE poetry to refer to kings and dynasties. Scholars suggest that Yngvi might refer to the Swedes and Norwegians, who are often called "Yngvi's people."

In the introduction to the *Prose Edda*, Snorri presents a version of history that says Odin was a powerful leader from Asia who traveled north into SCANDINAVIA and made many of his sons rulers in the lands he conquered. Yngvi was the son who became king of SWEDEN after Odin (see SAEMING).

**YUKI** See BIL AND YUKI.

# Selected Bibliography

GENERAL BOOKS ON MYTHOLOGY

Barber, Richard. *A Companion to World Mythology.* New York: Delacorte Press, 1979.

Bulfinch, Thomas. *Bulfinch's Mythology.* 1913. Reprint, New York: Modern Library, 1998.

Cotterell, Arthur. *A Dictionary of World Mythology.* Oxford/New York: Oxford University Press, 1990.

Frazer, James G. *The Golden Bough.* 1890. Reprint, New York: Wordsworth, 2001.

Gaster, Theodore H., ed. *The New Golden Bough: A New Abridgement of the Classic Work by Sir James George Frazer.* New York: Criterion Books, 1959.

Mercatante, Anthony S. *Facts On File Encyclopedia of World Mythology and Legend.* New York: Facts On File, 1989, 2003.

*New Larousse Encyclopedia of Mythology.* Trans. Richard Aldington and Delano Ames. London/New York: Hamlyn, 1968.

BOOKS ON NORSE MYTHOLOGY

Branston, Brian. *Gods and Heroes from Viking Mythology.* New York: Schocken Books, 1982.

———. *Gods of the North.* New York: Thames & Hudson, 1980.

Crossley-Holland, Kevin. *Axe-Age, Wolf-Age.* New York: E. P. Dutton, 1986.

———. *The Norse Myths.* New York: Random House, 1981.

D'Aulaire, Ingri, and Edgar Parin D'Aulaire. *D'Aulaire's Norse Gods and Giants.* 1967. Reprint, New York: Delacorte, 1986.

Davidson, H. R. Ellis. *Gods and Myths of Northern Europe.* New York: Viking Press, 1990.

———. *Pagan Scandinavia.* New York: Frederick A. Praeger, 1967.

———. *Scandinavian Mythology.* New York: Peter Bedricks Books, 1986.

DuBois, Thomas. *Nordic Religions in the Viking Age.* Philadelphia: University of Pennsylvania Press, 1999.

Fitzhugh, William W., and Elisabeth I. Ward, eds. *Vikings: The North Atlantic Saga.* Washington, D.C.: Smithsonian Institution Press, 2000.

Green, Roger Lancelyn. *Myths of the Norsemen.* 1960. Reprint, New York: Viking Press, 1988.

Grimm, Jakob. *Teutonic Mythology.* 7th ed. New York: Routledge, 2000.

Guerber, Helene A. *Myths of the Norsemen.* 1909. Reprint, New York: Dover Publications, 1992.

Lindow, John. *Handbook of Norse Mythology.* Santa Barbara, Calif. ABC-CLIO: 2001.

Orchard, Andy. *Dictionary of Norse Myth and Legend.* London: Cassell, 1997.

Paige, R. I. *Norse Myths.* Austin: University of Texas Press, 1991.

Snorri Sturluson. *The Prose Edda: Tales from Norse Mythology.* Trans. Jean I. Young. Berkeley: University of California, 2002.

Strayer, Joseph Reese, ed. *Dictionary of the Middle Ages.* New York: Scribner, 1989.

Turville-Petre, E. O. G. *Myth and Religion of the North.* Westport, Conn.: Greenwood Publishing, 1975.

# INDEX

Page numbers in **boldface** indicate main entries; page numbers in *italic* indicate illustrations and photographs